10
Principles
Of
Good
Design
Today

ARTPOWER

This book was originally conceived, written, and designed by Agata Toromanoff / Fancy Books Packaging. www.fancy-books-packaging.com

English edition © Artpower International Publishing Co. Ltd, 2021.
Original text and layout © Agata Toromanoff / Fancy Books Packaging

The Ten Principles of Good Design by Dieter Rams, which served as an inspirational source for this book, can be shared accurately and fairly under the Creative Commons CC-BY-NC-ND 4.0 licence.

10 PRINCIPLES OF GOOD DESIGN TODAY

Copyright © Artpower International Publishing Co., Ltd.

ARTPOWER

Publisher: Lu Jican
Chief Editor: Li Aihong, Wang Chen
Executive Editor: Shen Minping, Zhou Ziqing
Art Designer: Chen Ting, Xiong Libo

Registered Address
Flat A, 15/F, Goldfield Industrial Building, 144-150 Tai Lin Pai Road Kwai Chung, NT, Hong Kong, China
Tel: 852-21142801
Fax: 852-21142802

Editorial Department
Address: 5021-5023, 5th Floor, Phase II of Art Design Center, Zhanyi Road, Luohu District, Shenzhen, China
Tel: 86-755-25111140
Fax: 86-755-82020029

Web: www.artpower.com.cn / www.acs.cn
Sales & Distribution: overseasales@artpower.com.cn
Press & Editorial Submissions: press@artpower.com.cn / contact@artpower.com.cn

ISBN 978-988-75069-5-9

All Rights Reserved. No part of this publication may be reproduced or utilised in any form by any means, electronic or mechanical, including photocopying, recording or by any information storage and retrieval system, without prior written permission of the publisher.

All images in this book have been reproduced with the knowledge and prior consent of the designers and the clients concerned, and every effort has been made to ensure that credits accurately comply with information applied. No responsibility is accepted by producer, publisher, or printer for any infringement of copyright or otherwise arising from the contents of this publication.

Printed and bound in China.

10 PRINCIPLES OF GOOD DESIGN TODAY

AGATA TOROMANOFF

GOOD DESIGN* ...

IS INNOVATIVE	MAKES A PRODUCT USEFUL	IS AESTHETIC	MAKES A PRODUCT UNDERSTANDABLE	IS UNOBTRUSIVE
006 MLADEN HOYSS AND ADHAM BADR	028 NENDO	052 DECHEM STUDIO	074 CONSTANCE GUISSET	096 ANDERSSEN & VOLL
008 YVES BÉHAR	032 EVANGELOS VASILEIOU	054 NOÉ DUCHAUFOUR-LAWRANCE	076 CHRISTIAN WERNER	098 INGA SEMPÉ
010 NEWDEALDESIGN	034 HEATHERWICK STUDIO	056 STUDIO ORIJEEN	078 SOU FUJIMOTO	100 KONSTANTIN GRCIC
012 NATIVE UNION	036 SWNA	058 MONICA FÖRSTER	080 CECILIE MANZ	102 NEW TENDENCY
014 NICHETTO STUDIO	038 GAMFRATESI	060 PATRICIA URQUIOLA AND FEDERICO PEPE	082 TOMAS KRAL	104 JULIEN DE SMEDT
016 YUUE	040 CONSTANTINOS HOURSOGLOU	062 TOMÁS ALONSO	084 GUILLAUME DELVIGNE	106 JASPER MORRISON
018 EOOS	042 PHILIPPE NIGRO	064 FRONT	086 EMANUELE MAGINI	108 JEHS+LAUB
020 LENA SALEH	044 ARIK LEVY	066 FORMAFANTASMA	088 MICHAEL SODEAU	110 HARRI KOSKINEN
022 PAULINE DELTOUR	046 KEISUKE KAWASE	068 NERI & HU	090 SHANE SCHNECK	112 MARTIN ERICSSON
024 SIMPLEHUMAN	048 MINIMALUX	070 NATHALIE DU PASQUIER	092 CLARA VON ZWEIGBERGK	114 HENRIK PEDERSEN

*As defined by Dieter Rams

IS HONEST	IS LONG-LASTING	IS THOROUGH DOWN TO THE LAST DETAIL	IS ENVIRONMENTALLY-FRIENDLY	IS AS LITTLE DESIGN AS POSSIBLE
118 JAIME HAYON	140 FRANÇOIS AZAMBOURG	162 LARA BOHINC	184 JIN JURAMOTO	208 BERNHARDT & VELLA
120 CHARLOTTE JUILLARD	142 NORM ARCHITECTS	164 THOMAS BENTZEN	186 ATELIER MENDINI	210 RONAN & ERWAN BOUROULLEC
122 HELLA JONGERIUS	144 NORMAL STUDIO	166 DOSHI LEVIEN	190 SUPER LOCAL	212 NIKA ZUPANC
124 AYTM	146 BOWER STUDIOS	168 ANNE BOYSEN	192 ADIDAS DESIGN TEAM	214 SEBASTIAN HERKNER
126 THOMAS BERNSTRAND + LINDAU & BORSELIUS	148 DAVID ADJAYE	170 SCHOLTEN & BAIJINGS	194 MARJAN VAN AUBEL	216 CLAESSON KOIVISTO RUNE
128 STEFAN DIEZ	150 SMARIN	172 ALDO BAKKER	196 DOTE	218 LAYER / BENJAMIN HUBERT
130 MATALI CRASSET	152 E15	174 TADAO ANDO	198 ADAM SAVAGE	222 EDWARD BARBER & JAY OSGERBY
132 ROGER VANCELLS	154 TOM DIXON	176 SOVRAPPENSIERO DESIGN STUDIO	200 KARIM RASHID	224 MICHAËL VERHEYDEN
134 MARC VENOT AND ANTOINE LESUR	156 ROBIN HEATHER & KAI LINKE	178 ELISA STROZYK	202 BRIAN SIRONI	226 DAVID MELLOR
136 MARK DAY	158 PIETRO RUSSO	180 CRISTINA CELESTINO	204 RYAN MARIO YASIN	228 PATRICIA URQUIOLA

"Design for me is not about pandering to luxury buying incentives, but producing orientation and behavioural systems for a complex and complicated, yet simultaneously fascinating, open world. It is about seriously considering how to make this world a place where we can offer a tomorrow worth living for everyone." Dieter Rams, 2013

Dieter Rams' design sensibility has inspired many designers as well as design afcionados for many years. Designers are drawn by the clarity and functionality of his designs, while afcionados are seduced by their practical and aesthetical order. Rams' designs have been subjects of a careful consideration and not only respond to the needs of our lives today, but also protect the natural environment. The main objectives of products should be durability, usefulness and a human interface that offers a feeling of comfort in a rapidly changing world. Design for Rams is not a "fashionable ritual of aestheticism", but a contribution to make everyday life easier. It is for this reason he based his design process, in large part, on the basis of a dialogue with users in order to effectively address their requirements. In other words, the challenges that design should solve have been at the core of his practice. Last but not least, it is essential for the designer to create design that "overcomes thoughtless consumerism".

The designer's *Ten Principles for Good Design* (translated by some as commandments!) were put together in 1995, although the first attempts to theorize his design philosophy date back to the 1970s. These ten concise points are key milestones in the history of modern design, of which Rams is admittedly a pillar. His work, mainly for the electronics manufacturer Braun, contributed to the discipline's evolution. It expanded rapidly and changed dramatically over the more than 50 years of Rams' professional career. Design is a crucial, if not indispensable, part of today's life. And as remarked by one of the most influential and talented designers of today, Jonathan Ive: "We are at the beginning of a remarkable time, when a remarkable number of products will be developed. When you think about technology and what it has enabled us to do so far, and what it will enable us to do in future, we're not even close to any kind of limit."*

620 Chair Programme
by Dieter Rams for
Vitsoe, three-seat sofa
©Vitsoe

While design is more important than ever before, the debate about good design seems to be ignored in the press, which tends to promote the creations themselves rather than discussing their input. We suggest reinitiating the discussion by taking a closer look at one hundred outstanding designs by one hundred contemporary designers, both established and emerging, to see how they strive, to paraphrase Rams, to make tomorrow worth living. Do they come up with innovative solutions or just create trends? Are they focused on delivering design that genuinely improves our everyday life or only care about international hype? Do they take risks to push the boundaries of the discipline or follow the beaten path? While what constitutes good design usually remains open to individual interpretation, why not examine some of the latest creations to look for a kind of definition? Ten principles seem to provide a perfect litmus test for this purpose. "For me," states Dieter Rams, "good design is innovative, useful, aesthetic, understandable, unobtrusive, honest, durable, thorough to the last details, concerned with the environment and, last but not least, achieved with as little design as possible." What about the designers of today?

*In an interview with John Arlidge for *The Sunday Times*

#1

GOOD DESIGN IS INNOVATIVE

"The possibilities of innovation offered by new technologies are far from being exhausted. Technological progress will always offer new opportunities for pioneering design. Yet innovative design always works in tandem with new technology, and can never be an end in itself."

Dieter Rams

Dieter Rams' career spanned several decades that were marked by ground-breaking innovations. Today, as never before, we know that the boundaries of technological development are being constantly pushed further. Innovation, with unprecedented speed, introduces advancements in our everyday lifestyle, thus highly influencing it. Such improvements in technology create a similar need for innovative design. Each should complement the other in a perfect balance. Design should make technological innovation easy to grasp, aesthetically pleasing and simply useful. Technological progress, thanks to design, should lead to better ways of living. Users should be able to use technology intuitively, as a natural addition to their standard of living. Nowadays, using new technologies in design is probably one of the most complex challenges ever. According to Rams, a designer's success here depends, in large part, on a continuous dialogue with people, to understand them well in order to design for them.

MLADEN HOYSS AND ADHAM BADR
BllocZero18, 2017 / Blloc

"Focused on simplicity" is the slogan associated with the Blloc smartphone designed by Mladen Hoyss and Adham Badr. This new-generation phone, which combines a power-saving operating system and efficient hardware, is characterized by its minimalist appearance. While it keeps the best traditions by offering the same practical functions as a traditional phone — the basic functions are actually little changed since the invention of the telephone. The device takes us a step forward into the future of communicating systems. A perfectly serviceable tool, it also delights with its aesthetically pure and classy shape. The visual aspect of the phone aims for focus, and similarly its operating system does not include any redundant elements or internal menus. Instead, all is fluid, simplified to the nth degree, and compact. This approach is also reflected in the designers' choice of an elegant colour palette. Their monochromatic design language is clearly in line with its other minimalist features. It also keeps battery consumption to a minimum. However, users can easily switch to colour.

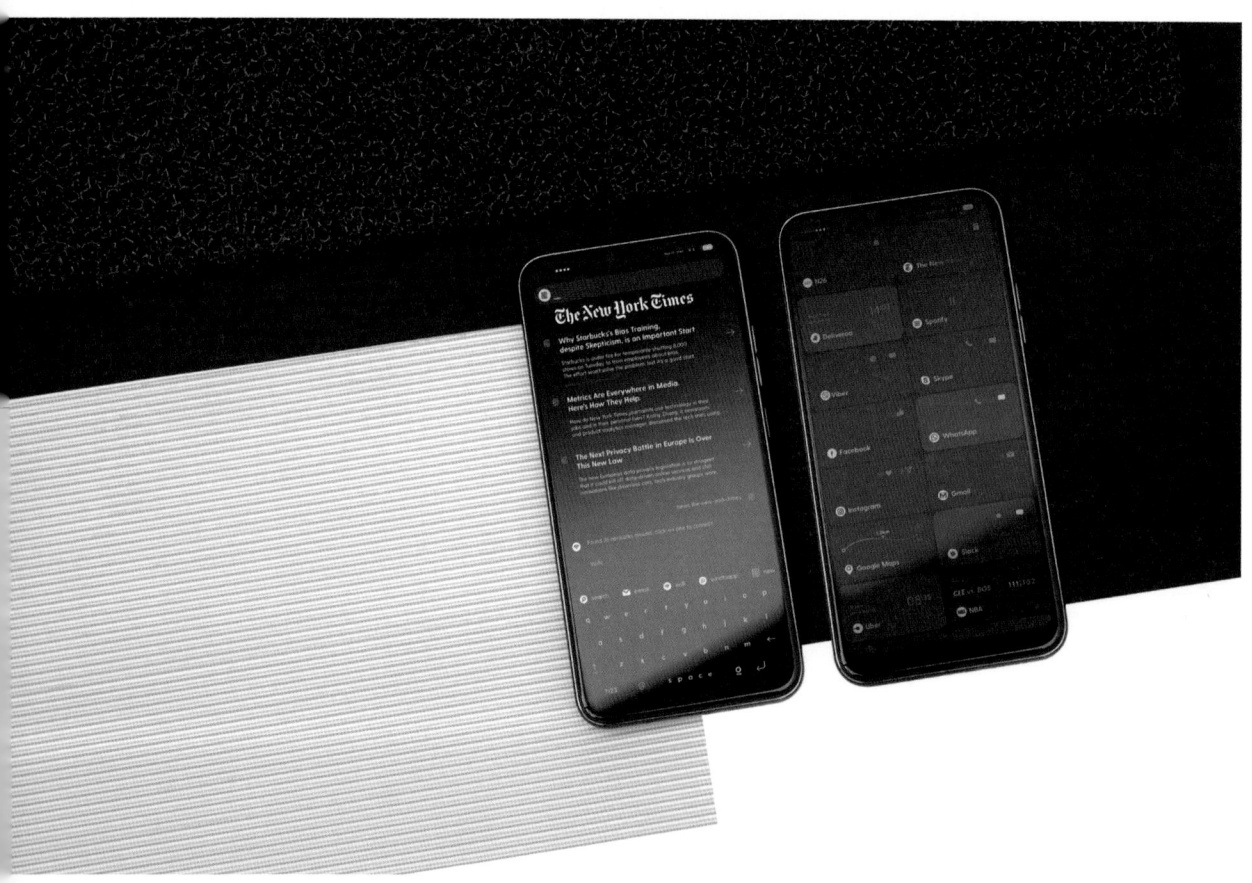

The main goal of the designer was to draw from the original and basic role of the phone, namely the way we interact with other people through it. Instead of implementing a number of superfluous features, to focus on the way we manage the contacts and messages. It is meant as an easily navigable communication tool that is elegant and handy at the same time. "Blloc comes with *Blloc* OS, a distraction-free custom operating system built on top of Android 8.1, which simplifes your dialogues and interactions by unifying all your application-scattered exchanges into a single timeline." explain the designers. Simplicity fuels their design philosophy, as they believe it should be at the core of innovation and business development. Although users are free to install any apps they wish, the most commonly used ones are already integrated into the Root, which covers all necessary actions from flight booking to wearther checking. Users can navigate easily between various features thanks to a well-considered layout, which is consistent with the pure shell. "Our device architecture is focused on the healthy balance between essential features and topnotch hardware." claim the designers. *Blloc* won the Silver A'Design Award in Digital and Electronic Devices Design Category in 2017.

YVES BÉHAR
Live OS, 2017 / Herman Miller

Swiss designer Yves Béhar is the CEO and founder of fuseproject, an award-winning industrial design and branding firm based in San Francisco. He is a design entrepreneur who believes that product, digital and brand designs are the cornerstones of any business. Together with his team, he works on a wide range of projects from fashion design to furniture. His impressive portfolio shows an emphasis put on the newest technologies and innovative solutions.

Among many other collaborations, the firm's partnership with Herman Miller has lasted over a decade and brought many interesting innovations into the workplace. The latest one is an intelligent office system called *Live OS*. As with previous common projects, it explores the role of technology in the office. "The aim is to answer the question of what happens when our workplace becomes intelligent — how can this benefit both the employee and the company?" asks the designer. As our working habits mainly involve sedentary positions, the major goal of *Live OS* is to promote physical activity as much as to enhance the functionality of the office space. How do Béhar and his team envision an intelligent office? The concept was developed to encourage regular changes of posture from sitting to standing and back again. An interactive desk controller includes special sensors in both the desk and the chair, which react to movements, or their lack, in one's body. Connected with the *Live OS* app, which also gathers personal preferences and habits, the system sends alerts through a gentle vibration in the desk and discreetly lighting up. To change the working position, it is enough to touch an easily reachable module that will modify the level of the height-adjustable desk and accommodate personalized needs. The system is highly flexible and goes beyond the reshaping of individual workspace. Within an office environment, when employees approach a shared desk, they only need to put their smartphones near the desk module and their presence will be automatically recognized via Bluetooth. It might be surprising to be reminded to change one's working position by a smartphone, but this innovative approach to office furniture transforms the working experience and initiates a virtuous chain reaction — becoming more active also makes employees more creative, healthier and happier.

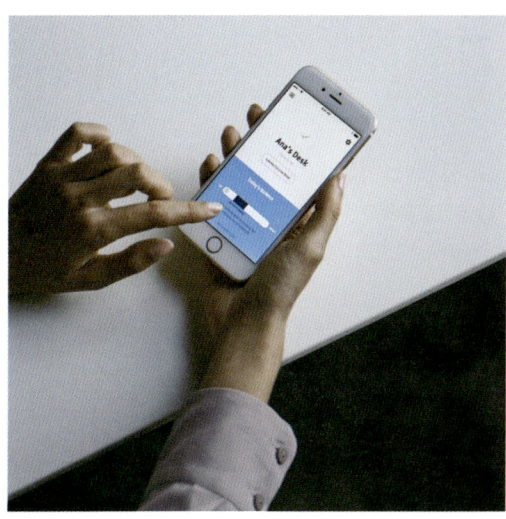

NEWDEALDESIGN
Spot, 2019

NewDealDesign demonstrates how to successfully marry digital technology and education. Spot, their concept project envisioned by Tony Smith (Industrial Design) and Stephanie Lee (Experience Design), employs artificial intelligence. It is a prototype of a one-of-a-kind tool to inspire children (suggested ages 5–9) to explore the natural world. Easy to grasp, the durable device consists of a 3D-camera that detects objects in real time and a pico projector. All you have to do is point it at a selected object and wait until Spot recognises it. Once an object is spotted, it starts speaking to the little explorer, sharing some information about itself. The youngster simply becomes friends with living creatures and plants. The process trains the child's observation skills as it requires focus and a bit of patience, both valuable in today's speedy world. This ingenious digital companion in the educational process has yet another surprising function. In the evening, after an adventurous day, Spot can connect all of the objects and project a narrative "bedtime story" onto a wall of a child's room. It is fun for children to see themselves in the main role of a movie, made from their own exploration history.

The storytime mode is also a great way to wind down and to reinforce newly gained knowledge. Additionally, as the creators emphasize, "It turns out that contextualizing the world with stories about themselves as the focal point helps self-confidence and self-awareness".

Young users not only learn words or facts but they can also put them together to form a bigger picture of the natural world. Importantly, Spot adjusts to each child's pace and supports their interests. This learning-by-doing approach invites youngsters to be actively curious and gives them a fanciful tool that makes learning and playing one and the same. The idea of engaging children with their natural surroundings was the designer's main goal. Another was to train children's rapidly dwindling attention spans. As a result, this technology stimulates and helps users slow down rather than overloading them with images or overwhelming them with screen environments. NewDealDesign convincingly affirms that "Being 'present' and 'in-the-moment' is a skill that can be taught".

San Francisco-based NewDealDesign led by Gadi Amit specializes in using advanced technologies to, as they say, "build joyful digital and physical experiences". The brand collaborates with numerous clients internationally, but also works on their own highly innovative concept product projects.

NATIVE UNION
Watch DOCK / Native Union

The *Watch DOCK* by Native Union is yet more proof that practical objects can be visually stunning. This innovative charger for the Apple Watch is a must-have for anyone who likes to be up-to-date with the newest technologies. Meant as a sturdy platform, not only for charging but also for navigating the device, it is compatible with all models, sizes and strap styles. Last but not least, it is a great idea for displaying the watch, and a safer way of re-charging it instead of letting it lie on a table. The minimal base is built without any screws; the two components simply snap together magnetically. The *DOCK* has a reversible design, which means that the watch can be charged in either a horizontal or a vertical position. Users simply turn the base over and position the rotating arm on either side. It provides easy access to the watch's face. This option is particularly convenient for left-handed people or the moment when one moves the base within a room. The thought behind the design of the *DOCK* is that users typically re-charge their watches during the night; the device can be easily transformed into a bedside alarm clock. "When the *DOCK* is in its horizontal position, the device that is being recharged will automatically switch to nightstand mode. It gives an easier access to see the illuminated screen and to operate all functions including turning off or snoozing the alarm." explain the designers. It is obviously much more than a bedside clock as users can easily access all the other options as well.

Featured here is an exceptionally solid marble edition. Cut from solid marble and polished by hand, each one is unique due to the veins in the material's structure. In this versatile object, innovative technology meets with a stylish look and the finest quality of classical material. While the *DOCK* showcases and charges the Apple Watch, it is an elegant piece of design in its own right. Its sleek form draws attention to the watch, which can be easily used while "docking".

NICHETTO STUDIO
Astro, 2018 / Tubes

    Astro is both an ingenious fan heater and an efficient air purifier at the same time. It is adaptable for any environment. "Heat and air, two primary needs for the human being, represent the essence of this object, which contains the technology required to independently perform two functions: heating and purifying." comments the manufacturer, the Italian brand Tubes. Flexibility fuels not only the functional aspect, but also the visual side of the design. Made with a polyurethane shell and available in several vivid colours, *Astro* is standardly equipped with two sets of legs of different heights. Depending on the character of the interior, its height can be easily transformed into a higher or lower version. In either case, it easily becomes a furnishing element thanks to its intriguing yet discreet look. "Designed as a small spaceship that is about to take off, the *Astro* fan heater can explore and land in various places in the home or the office", as the designers describe it. To make the device more functional, its primary heating function is enhanced by the technology of air purification. This way, the device can be used all year round. *Astro*'s innovative character does not end here. While there are buttons on the body to activate the device or adjust its intensity, the device can also be controlled remotely through Bluetooth and a dedicated app, which multiplies the number of functions. *Astro* is part of the manufacturer's new *Plug&Play* collection, which focuses on heating objects free of installation constraints. The idea is to challenge the static nature of objects and architecture to "open up to the human dimension which by definition, is in constant movement and evolution", as the statement reads.

Luca Nichetto founded his design studio back in 2006. Based in Venice and Stockholm (the second office opened in 2011), his multidisciplinary team conceives and executes numerous projects for international brands. The studio's projects are renowned for their attention to detail and interesting references. The *Astro*'s design team includes Francesco Dompieri and Jean Montfort.

YUUE
Tangible Memory

      The Berlin-based design studio YUUE, established in 2015 by Weng Xinyu and Tao Haiyue (both graduated in product design at the Bauhaus University in Weimar), is renowned for designing extraordinary products that look like objects of everyday life, yet with unexpected, additional features. Whether the duo designs lighting, furniture, accessories or electric appliances and more, the focus is always on exploring the human-object relationship with a strong emphasis on interactivity and emotion. YUUE's *Tangible Memory* is a very interesting example of an object created with an emotional dimension. Made of sheet metal and glass, it looks rather inconspicuous. But after a long time, if left untouched, the framed photo will blur, alluding to the idea that it simply fades away, like a memory itself being forgotten. If the user touches the photo frame, the glass will slowly become clear to reveal the image again. While it delivers a poetic and emotional message, it also requires a response from the user. The latter somehow makes the object complete. Conceived as an interpretation of time and memory, this is probably the most original photo frame

in the world. The product requires continual interaction to cause the frame to play its function. By doing so it enhances the very idea of capturing memories in the photos we later frame. This innovative design encourages the user to cherish and contemplate memories and past moments, which gives the design both an emotional and lyric facet. YUUE's inventive technology leads to an innovative, human-centred approach to design. An object is not merely an element fulfilling its role, but an interactive tool, which functions properly only with the user's action. At the same time, YUUE's well-thought-out concepts touch upon the essence of things.

YUUE's founder, China-born designer Weng Xinyu exemplifies a fresh, original perception of modern design. While he seeks inspiration by comparing his cultural background with daily life at the moment, as he states, the focus of his research aims at understanding the relationship between mankind and its creations. Design is for him a way to define contemporary aesthetics and also to explore the future principles of product design, as Xinyu defines it.

EOOS
Nuki, 2017 / NUKI

EOOS was founded in 1995 by three graduates from the University of Applied Arts in Vienna — Gernot Bohmann, Harald Gründl and Martin Bergmann. Based in the Austrian capital, the award-winning team operates in the fields of furniture and product design, as well as shop design. "For EOOS, design is a poetical discipline between archaic and high-tech", reads the statement. "EOOS examines rituals, myths and intuitive images as a starting point within the scope of the Poetical Analysis®." the studio adds.

All projects in the EOOS portfolio are far from typical or boring. Innovation and a fresh approach to solving problems are the driving forces behind their concepts. *NUKI* ("New Key") marks a cutting-edge moment in the team's career as it is the first robot designed by EOOS. The installation of this electronic door lock could not be easier. Mounted on top of an existing door cylinder on the inside of the entrance door (no need for drilling or any screws), it is controlled through an app. *NUKI* has been designed to take over opening and closing the doors, it just turns the mechanical key and pulls the latch when someone approaches. The LED ring (the same feature as in the app) indicates whether the door is closed or open: a closed circle means a locked door. The status can be checked at any time on a smartphone and one can also manage access permission for guests (the lock is also meant as a solution for shared spaces).

A little Bluetooth device on a key ring also enables the user to lock or unlock the door without a smartphone. In case of an emergency, the outer circle at the top of the lock allows the door to be opened manually. Each lock can manage up to 100 permissions, the underpinning is end-to-end encryption with security standards comparable to those of the online banking sector. Although EOOS drew inspiration for the design of the user's interface from the aesthetic workmanship and symbolic character of old locks, their *NUKI*, as an innovative and smart door access system, makes keys (especially the lost ones) a thing of the past.

LENA SALEH
Sleep Kit Breath Lux Light & Roma Olfacto, 2017

Lena Saleh, who graduated from Central Saint Martins with a Master of Art in material futures, focuses on product design, interiors, materials and visually stimulating digital applications. Her *Sleep Kit* is a set of objects that revolutionize the way we sleep. The pace of contemporary life, the omnipresence of technology affecting our body's natural rhythms, and more frequent travels across time zones, have negatively impacted our quality of sleep. "Researchers have coined the 'glymphatic system' as the brain's garbage disposal, removing all the toxins that have built up throughout the day." Saleh explains. "When sleep is deprived or even disturbed, the glymphatic system does not have time to perform its function and toxins build up, which could lead to Lena

Saleh neurodegenerative diseases." she adds. Trying to solve this serious issue, the designer created a collection of products, we can interact with before falling asleep as an alternative to looking at the glowing screens of our smartphones, TVs or computers.

The objects' main goal is to encourage mindful breathing rituals based on pranayama technique. Saleh places a functional tool into a visually intriguing shape that has a sculptural presence. The tool's mission is to wind down the user through simple and short sensory experiences using scent and light to create a new night-time routine, as rituals should be a crucial part of daily life. Promoting healthy habits is an essential part of the collection's agenda. Implemented in a smart home, the objects from the collection are able to technologically track the sleep pattern, and also adjust the environment by lowering the room's temperature or changing the light level. While the *Breath Lux Light* encourages the user to undertake breathing exercises with the use of soft lighting, the *Roma Olfacto* diffuser emits scents to enhance our mindfulness and well-being. Speaking of her inspirations, Saleh mentions the exploring sleep temples in ancient Egypt, where people received healing from their ailments. Her product aims to aid sleep, improve the quality of our sleep, which also improves our everyday functioning. As we are currently obsessed with various devices and technology in general, interacting with Saleh's *Sleep Kit* can be a mind-opening experience.

PAULINE DELTOUR
Monimalz, 2017
Yellow Innovation / La Poste

    Pauline Deltour is a young French designer, a graduate of art and design at the Olivier de Serres (ENSAAMA) and in industrial design from the École Nationale Supérieure des Arts Décoratifs (ENSAD), both in Paris. She started her career as a designer and project leader at the Konstantin Grcic's studio in Munich. Currently based in Paris, Deltour has run her own practice since 2009 and works on a wide range of projects spanning industrial products and furniture to jewellery and public spaces.
    Deltour's ingenious *Monimalz* collection takes saving money to a new level. This 21st century piggy bank functions as an online banking system. Designed for Yellow Innovation / La Poste, it is a new generation moneybox that is intelligently connected to the kids' bank accounts. The series shares the same smooth and minimal shape, but Deltour designed several interchangeable magnetic masks featuring a panda, a monkey or a whale, which can become guardians of the savings. These finishing details, added to the main body, look really cute and can be easily replaced. The moneybox can be also personalized with stickers available for various

ages, so that the device can grow together with the kids. Thanks to a screen on the belly, children can always check their current balance, or see when they receive money or messages. *Monimalz* is connected to a mobile app enabling family members or friends to transfer money into the account easily, using their bank card details or through bank transfers. Interestingly, it also accepts coins, thus bridging the traditional idea of a piggy bank with the newest technology. When a coin is added, the saving pet comes to life by showing the value of the coin and adding it to the existing savings balance. An option for sending messages that scroll across the *Monimalz* is another innovative feature. It lights up with funny animations and sounds. Donors can send wishes or set tasks, which, if fulfilled, will gain additional pocket money. The app controlling the device is still under development, and will expand even further to teach children how to save and manage money. Invented as a smart and fun friend, *Monimalz* is an educational tool, but it is also a stylish decorative element for the children's room.

SIMPLEHUMAN
ST2015, 2018

Throwing away rubbish has entered the 21st century. *Simplehuman* introduces "a more civilized trash can" that offers a more efficient recycling system. The California-based brand, specializing in smart solutions for bath and kitchen, developed a sensor technology that provides the users with much quicker and more hygienic access to the bin. The main innovation here is that the bin is equipped with voice and motion control. Smart sensors adapt to the surrounding environment and, as the producer assures, do not react to false instructions. Whether to the command "open can" or in response to the wave of a hand, the lid opens up to a space-efficient dual compartment to sort our recyclables and trash conveniently. The reaction of the system is immediate and there is no need to remove the top or even touch the surface.

An easy-to-remove plastic bucket on one side is meant for recycling, while a second compartment is for the trash. As soon as the rubbish lands inside the bin, it closes automatically over the liner. The sleek design of this newest bin concept includes a powerful yet small and quiet motor, which fits into the hinge. Thanks to this, the bin's lid is lifted gently and does not need much space. It can stand next to the wall. The designers created an innovative solution in an elegant and minimalist silhouette, which can easily be a free-standing kitchen accessory. Additionally, the *ST2015* is made of stainless steel and is covered with an invisible fingerprint-proof coating infused with nano-silver particles. The goal is to prevent microbes from reproducing. It makes the bin look clean and sleek. As an even more practical feature, the designers included an innovative liner pocket inside the bin that stores and dispenses custom-fit and extremely durable liners to make changing liners faster and easier. Transforming trash-duty into a "hands-free" experience is achieved here in an extremely elegant way. Its ingenious design and innovative functionality earn *ST2015* the title of smart bin.

#2

GOOD DESIGN MAKES A PRODUCT USEFUL

"A product is bought to be used. It has to match certain criteria, not only of functional, but also of psychological and aesthetic nature. Good design emphasizes the usefulness of a product whilst disregarding anything that could possibly detract from it."

Dieter Rams

Utility has long been the subject of debate in modern design. In the duel between function and aesthetics, it is not always obvious to tell who the winner is. Some designers pay attention exclusively to the way a product can be useful to users, and the aesthetic aspect is less of an issue, or at least doesn't play the main role. Others, on the contrary, cherish the look rather than the practical features, and select what they regard as beautiful even if the utilitarian element is not that strong. Ideally, not only both factors should be perfectly balanced, but also — to paraphrase Dieter Rams — the utility should be revealed by the design without dominating the scene. While using products, we should enjoy their visual aspect as much as their functional one, even if the first one should naturally express the latter. Today's designers harmonize both aspects expertly.

NENDO
Totte-plate, 2015 / by | n

Established by Japanese designer Oki Sato, Nendo is one of the most interesting voices of design today. The studio is renowned for outside-the-box designs that are visually stunning. As they describe their mission, the goal is to give people "!" moments. "We'd like the people who've encountered Nendo's designs to feel these small '!' moments intuitively." they say. Among many other highly diversified realizations (the studio's portfolio amounts to 400 projects), Nendo also designed a collection of ceramic tableware. The approach to the task was unconventional, in line with Nendo's tradition: creating a product for small-size living spaces as the main idea behind the concept. Re-thinking the way we use dishes is driven by the lack of space, a phenomenon observed in all metropolises. Nendo's *Totte-plate* is not only practical to store, but also easy to carry.

The handle is the hallmark of the series. Typically, and unlike cooking utensils like pots or pans, tableware does not have handles. Nendo decided not to take this for granted, and added a single handle ("totte" in Japanese) to each plate and bowl to empower them with new functions. They are easier to carry, they can be hung and stored with hooks, and are easier to hold when the plates and bowls are hot. Not only has this resulted in new ways of using them, but has also provided them with a strong "sense of security as a tool", the studio comments. The collection includes round plates and bowls. Each of them comes in three different sizes, which creates a perfect basic set, and the five colours can be used and arranged in interesting combinations. The rectangular handles are perfectly integrated with the circular form of the tableware. Extending from the rim, they are a perfect solution for avoiding burnt fingers when the plates are hot. The dishes don't have to be stored in a cupboard, they only need a hook on a wall, which is convenient in compact interiors. On top of their practical use, with their simple design and sophisticated colour palette when the plates are hung on the wall they are decorative.

EVANGELOS VASILEIOU
Nolly, 2017 / Ligne Roset

Nolly combines legs made of solid, black-stained ash with two overlapping tops. While the lower top is fixed, the upper, much thicker one, can rotate. This is technically possible thanks to a double disc and a ball-bearing assembly. Contrasting colours play another interesting role in the design. The movable top is available in grey or lavender, and either works well in contrast with the dark base, and results in visual lightness. When fully opened, the upper top is suspended in the air. With the top's subtle hues, this effect is enhanced visually. What is striking in this low coffee table is its great sense of proportion. Whether the table is fully opened or not, it has a very harmonious look, and makes a perfect solution for small spaces: In a compact position, it doesn't occupy much space, but when the users need more surface space, they can simply swivel open the upper circular top (the overall width is nearly 90 centimetres). The table is very handy, as this transformation is easy and quick. Both configurations please the eye, however, the fully opened one adds a playful element to the interior. Floating over the ground and somehow also over a more typical looking table construction, the rotating disc looks surreal. One gets the impression that the construction

has lost its balance and will collapse, especially because the movable top differs significantly in thickness. Designed for Ligne Roset, *Nolly* is an elegant addition to any space. It successfully satisfies all criteria, whether functional, psychological or aesthetic. Moreover, the well-proportioned and chic design enhances its practical use. The style is universal enough to match various styles of sofas or armchairs.

    Athens-born, and Paris-based designer Evangelos Vasileiou graduated in both architecture and product design. In 2005, together with Aurélie Cristofari, he co-founded a practice specializing in architectural and interior projects (two years later the designer established another office in Athens). Characteristic of, and common to, Vasileiou's furniture designs is an interesting mix of great proportions, modern silhouettes with a retro feel.

HEATHERWICK STUDIO
Friction Table, 2017

London-based and internationally renowned Heatherwick Studio is responsible for originating numerous ingenious designs, including the New Route master, the latest version of the famous red double-decker bus the London streets are famous for. The team gathers "180 problem solvers dedicated to making the physical world around us better for everyone", as the statement reads. Working across disciplines, the studio's projects range from buildings and master-plans to infrastructure and objects. While projects with the greatest positive social impact are prioritized, the team's goal is not a signature style. "The approach driving everything is to lead from human experience rather than any fixed design dogma." they declare.

Called forward-thinking, the *Friction Table* is a very smart solution for limited spaces that accommodates any number of guests at a dinner party or a business meeting. The flexibility of this unusual table is its main quality. It uses a simple, mechanical device of the lattice with precise execution to change its proportions. Adapting to the needs in various spaces, and to multiple uses, the

table is made of sheets of paper solidified in resin. In its original, round configuration, it has a diameter of 1.8 metres, and can seat eight people. The table reaches over 4 metres when fully extended to an elliptical shape, and accommodates larger gatherings. The latticed structure, made of slats, is easy to extend, one only has to stretch it according to one's needs. Interestingly, the studio became interested in the idea of furniture with flexible proportions while the designers were thinking about another design issue. It was after experimenting with the pivot mechanism in a number of projects, and exploring various forms that they decided it should be used for an expanding table. The whole process took several years, and the table constructions involved precise engineering. However, as the studio stresses, the finishing process of the piece turns it into hand-crafted furniture. Finding inventive solutions, exploring materials and attention to detail during the making process are signature features of the Heatherwick Studio practice. *Friction Table*, which embodies them all, is the third piece in the studio's series of experimental design works. It was produced in a limited edition of 7.

SWNA
Life Clock, 2017 /
Korea Gyeonggido Company

Life Clock was conceived and designed to help people survive emergency situations. Its sleek body with rounded shapes actually contains a survival kit with tools to be used in the event of any natural disaster. The device was designed by SWNA, an industrial design studio established by Sukwoo Lee in Seoul in 2008. "We are an incredibly passionate group of specialists who strive to create meaningful design for a better world." says the team. "This means that we are not just one-dimensional designers but rather the three-dimensional thinkers, innovators and ground breakers." True to these principles, SWNA designed an object that can save one's life. The commissioning of a "disaster-related" product for the public came from the Korea Gyeonggido Company, and followed a series of natural catastrophes in the region.

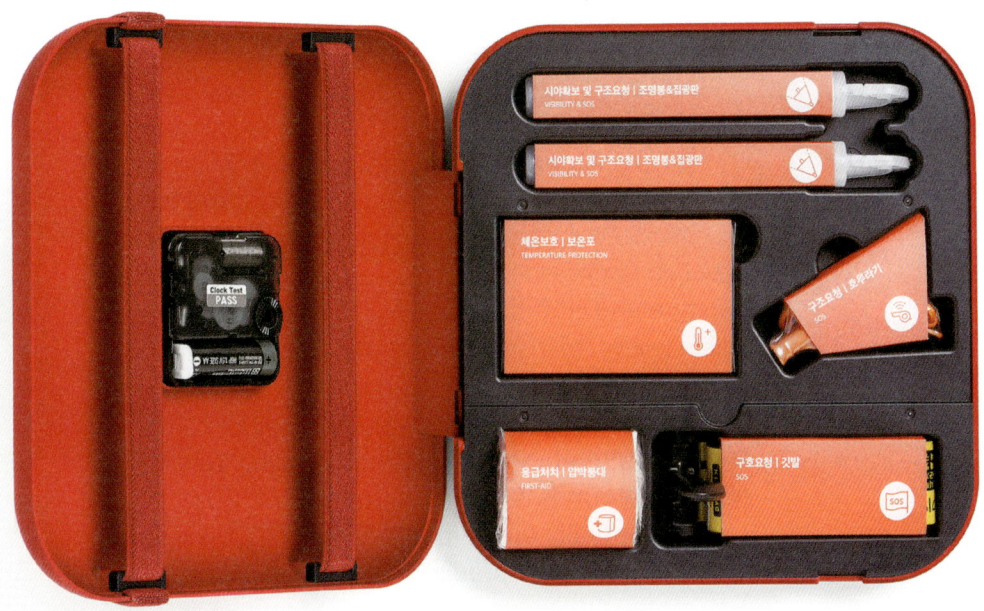

Dedicated to very special tasks, *Life Clock*, besides telling time, also includes an in-case-of-emergency card, a disaster and safety manual created in consultation with experts on disaster safety, some practical aid as well as emergency tools (including a torch, an aluminium heat blanket, a pressure pack, and a whistle). It is light and portable to be easily carried around. While the product is characterized by its added functionality, the design remains inconspicuous. *Life Clock* can easily become a stylish element of interior decoration with its minimal and contemporary look. Available in three colours, it is perfect for anyone who likes well-designed objects.

"We thought that it was important to recognise that disasters could happen to us and that it was important for disaster supplies to co-exist with our lives in everyday life rather than something special." comments Lee. By using a clock, which is an essential object in any space, the designers wanted to encourage people to be aware of the possibility of an emergency situation and to keep essential life-saving equipment handy at home. There is also another, more symbolic aspect of the project, which explains the selection of this particular object as the emergency kit holder: an object which tells the time is ideal when one is fighting against time when rescuing lives.

GAMFRATESI
Nubo Desk, 2013 / Ligne Roset

Danish architect Stine Gam and Italian architect Enrico Fratesi form a unique design duo. They founded studio GamFratesi in Copenhagen in 2006, and their exceptional design pieces are fueled by constant dialogue between their respective cultures. The classic Danish furniture and craft tradition meet here with the classic Italian intellectual and conceptual approach. While the duo's works reflect the mix of traditions, each object — be it an armchair, desk or lamp among others — is an original interpretation of this interbreeding. This fusion of dual backgrounds is extremely interesting, both visually and conceptually. In addition, GamFratesi's minimalist aesthetics and their predilection for experimenting with materials produce a sophisticated effect. It is also an ode to traditional craftsmanship. "GamFratesi aims to create furniture that illustrates the process and the techniques that created it, and which recflect a persistent exploration of the diverse border zone between harmony anddisharmony", reads the studio's statement.

For Ligne Roset, GamFratesi designed a space-saving wall desk. "For *NUBO*, an aesthetic awe comes from the unexpected encounter between the déjà-vuand a surprising new element: the simple space saving wall shelf transforms into precious box, reminiscent of a travel case, such as the Pan-Am blue case of the 1960s." describes the manufacturer. In an open position, *NUBO* generously offers space to work, as well as to store some items behind a special bracket. Closed, it gives additional space, while its external face, upholstered with Divina wool, decorates the wall in an original way. The sky-blue colour of the wool comes from a Scandinavian vintage registry. It also works well with the hue of the natural oak veneered beech plywood of the structure. Its shape also draws from retro chic with its rounded corners. The shell is practical and its structure creates a visually delightful contrast with the woolen upholstery thus showing the duo's sense of materials. Easy to open on two metallic folding supports and to close with magnetic catches, the desk is also equipped with a slot for inserting a cable. On the one hand, it is a functional workplace, and on the other hand, an object that is decorative and unusual.

CONSTANTINOS HOURSOGLOU
bOx, 2013 / Shibui

The Japanese word "*shibui*" refers to an aesthetic vision of simple, unobtrusive beauty. The Swiss-based brand was established by two Greek designers, Constantinos Hoursoglou and Athanasios Babalis, to produce homeware and accessories that would be both sustainable and simple. "To us, *shibui* means design in harmony with nature, where every form has a function and every detail a purpose." the founders claim. "Handmade in Europe by specialist artisans, our creations are inspired by a desire to make elegant, useful objects accessible to all." they add.

bOx, designed by Hoursoglou, is the best example of the label's philosophy. Like other designs using natural materials, it is made to last. It is a well thought out and highly practical modular box for jewellery or watches. While its central compartments are made to store rings, cufflinks and other small items, the middle part, which is reversible, can accommodate necklaces of different sizes, or watches. As such it is a perfect accessory for both men and women. Handmade with precision and with an eye for detail, *bOx* combines simplicity with usefulness. When closed, *bOx* becomes a compact object that is as decorative as the accessories hidden inside. The pure and simple silhouette of the container, splendidly executed in wood, celebrates natural beauty. Wood is also a perfect material for displaying jewellery in an elegant way. The designer plays with the proportions of the three box elements, which suggest a system of varying compartments inside and make the outside look more intriguing. Minimalist from the outside and complex inside, *bOx* offers a practical storage space for precious items. As harmonious geometry and natural material are key, its visibly high-quality comes from the fact that it uses artisan craftsmanship. Apart from its aesthetic and practical features, the design is also sustainable, which is one of the *Shibui* brand's most important values. Hoursoglou studied industrial design in the United Kingdom, where he graduated from the Royal College of Art. He worked for Karim Rashid, among others. 2002 marked the establishment of his own studio in his hometown of Athens, but since 2007 the designer has been based in Geneva.

PHILIPPE NIGRO
Dressoir à thé - Les Curiosités, 2014 / Hermès

"To consider the everyday through objects which are surprising, yet sensible" is Philippe Nigro's maxim. The renowned French designer studied decorative arts and product design. Since 1999 he has worked as an independent designer and also in collaboration with Michele De Lucchi, Italian architect and designer, with whom he realized many projects including lighting, furniture and interior design. "Characterized by a connection between prospective research and pragmatic appreciation of the 'savoir-faire' of manufacturers with whom he works, Philippe moves between projects of different scales, whether it is well-known brands, the luxury industry or local craftsmanship", reads the designer's statement.

Hermès, the French luxury-goods manufacturer, is famous for fruitful collaborations with leading designers. In 2014, the brand teamed up with Philippe Nigro to createthe series *Les Curiosités d'Hermès* interpreted by various designers over the years. One of the results is the *Dressoir à thé*. Nigro decided to create a classy cabinet for all items essential to celebrating a tea ceremony, including sets of cups, plates, pots and tins for various infusions. Cabinets of curiosities traditionally gathered collections of objects or specimens of particular categories, such as geology or ethnography. *Dressoir à thé* follows the same concept, but focuses on everyday objects namely elegant porcelain for drinking tea. When closed, the cabinet looks inconspicuous. Only after opening the double doors will the interior delight the eyes with numerous tiny shelves, dividers and drawers made to fit various shapes and sizes of cups, plates as well as to accommodate slightly bigger pieces of the set like a teapot, sugar bowl or a milk jug. The space is used extremely efficiently, and even the inside of the doors is part of the smart display. Each element of the complex, yet perfectly organized interior, was precisely planned. Nigro's cabinet is also a sophisticated balance of forms and muted colours. Although the proportions play the main role on the look of the outside, inside the designer makes perfect use of geometrical rhythms. In the same year Nigro designed another "abinet of curiosities", this time devoted to shoes. *Coffre à chaussures* is a comfortable and highly practical way to store footwear and all necessary accessories.

ARIK LEVY
Toolbox, 2010 / Vitra

Toolboxes are usually associated with a handyman's activity rather than being an accessory for the home or office. Arik Levy, however, recognized the practical potential of the object and decided to design one as a home accessory with a playful character. Manufactured by Vitra, it is available in a range of different colours to match any interior. The look is entirely based on a real toolbox with its easy-to-carry handle and rectangular shape. Inside, the toolbox offers countless compartments of various sizes for storing accessories as well as small items. The box organizes things for you. Levy's toolbox has compact dimensions and thus does not take up much space on a table or shelf. Moreover, it can be easily moved from one place to another. As a portable storage system, it is particularly helpful if one needs to use items in more than one room. The toolbox can, for instance, transform into a moveable office, carrying stationery and everything needed to run an errand. It can be a perfect container for kitchen utensils. It can, of course, also serve as storage for tools. It was never as easy to organize objects on one's desk, in a cabinet or workshop. The toolbox's look is appealing enough to be displayed, yet its practical size allows it to be stowed away in less exposed places. Levy's toolbox for Vitra

will prove an essential organizational support for any situation or space. Made of ABS plastic, it is easy to clean and visually attractive.

Tel-Aviv-born Levy studied industrial design at Art Center College of Design in La Tour-de-Peilz in Switzerland. In 1997, together with Pippo Lionni, he founded an independent studio in Paris called "L design". Levy works across disciplines and realizes a truly wide range of projects from sculptures and installations to industrial design and hi-tech clothing (interestingly, he also designs stage sets for modern dance productions). The designer's collaboration with Vitra, focused on office furnishings, has been evolving since 2000. The multidisciplinary character of Levy's practice results in out-of-the-box concepts in all fields.

KEISUKE KAWASE
Insideout, 2017

An emerging star of Japanese design scene, interior architect and designer, Keisuke Kawase, gained recognition for his playful ideas about organizing space. His signature use of geometric shapes introduces an interesting flow to the interiors. *Insideout* is a freestanding modular shelving system for an inviting and rhythmical arrangement of the space. It acts as a shelf and divider in one, thus adding to its functionality. The cubic shelves are stackable. Each unit consists of a wooden frame and a back panel. The interplay between the open and closed structures is enhanced by the rhythm of the divisions within the shelves. This structural division of space looks as if Kawase deconstructed a regular shelf by extracting its single units to allow individual arrangements depending on the particular needs of each interior.

As with many of the designer's projects, this one is about interaction with the user. Creating a relationship between the user and the furniture is, according to Kawase, a part of the design's goal because "it creates an affective value through the dialogue of the user and the furniture in the actual space". By combining the shelves in various configurations, each user can create their individual storing or dividing system, which can be easily modified in order to transform the space. It can be fully closed on one side and open on the other or arranged alternately to form a more complex freestanding structure. The width and height of the final shelf-partition is adjustable and only depends on the space it occupies. Last but not least, the arrangement can also be diversified through colour. Whether one prefers a monochromatic effect or a play of dark and bright hues, the units are available in green and beige. Contemporary interiors often require a very flexible and inventive approach. Partitions allow more efficient space management, especially in larger interiors like lofts or open space offices. Kawase's design offers many alternatives to building a wall. Another advantage is the storage capacity it provides, something that is always in high demand. Combining a divider with capacious shelves to stow various items doubles the practical value of *Insideout*.

MINIMALUX
Pill Tube, 2017

London-based brand *Minimalux* specializes in aesthetically stunning, minimalist objects. Simple designs and elegant materials are the label's recipe for refined pieces. "A minimal approach to form together with solid, lasting materials and impeccable finishing. We wanted to bring to the market a concept of luxury that wasn't based on opulence or decadence but substance and sound, timeless values." explains Mark Holmes who co-founded the brand together with Tamara Caspersz. *Minimalux* works with the best contemporary craftspeople, and their products are of the highest quality, due to the fact that they are hand-finished.

Minimalux's new take on everyday objects results in a number of beautiful, but also very useful products, among them is the *Pill Tube*. This portable vessel in the form of a test tube is handy in size: 100 x 16 x 16 mm. The shape and dimensions of the tube will fit a range of pills and it is also easy to carry. It is an indispensable companion for many of us, but a container for medications usually does not stand out aesthetically, and is usually hidden away by users. Here the object is transformed into a classy accessory available in natural or plated metal finishes. *Minimalux* focuses on delivering a product that reinvents the experience of taking pills. With a beautiful object like *Pill Tube*, carrying daily doses of medication with you becomes much more pleasant. The production of *Pill Tubes* is fascinating. They are electroformed of solid copper and mirror polished by hand. "They are literally grown from nothing in tanks of copper particles, each one takes a whole day to fully form." explains Holmes. A cork bung provides an airtight seal and adds a practical finish that visually contrasts with the body of the tube. It will efficiently prevent from any pills from falling out. The practical and aesthetic aspects are perfectly balanced in this design. What Holmes says about all of the label's products makes an excellent point about the *Pill Tube*, too: "They are not meant to take over, but merely 'season' your world with their shared common attributes. They are small objects that quietly make a big difference!"

#3

GOOD DESIGN IS AESTHETIC

"The aesthetic quality of a product is an integral part of its usefulness, because products, we use every day, affect our life and well-being. But only well-executed objects can be beautiful."

Dieter Rams

Usefulness can and should be aesthetic, as both criteria affect our relationship with any designed object. What we surround ourselves with directly influences our everyday lives. We feel well and confident when we know we can rely on the tools we use, as they support our existence efficiently by meeting our needs exactly. However, the aesthetic pleasure an object provides is no less important and complements the practical one. Aesthetics is not an end in itself, but when embracing the functional aspect of an object, it plays an essential role. It can animate our moods, regulate our pace of life, or even lower our levels of stress. Interiors filled with designs that are all simple, tasteful and useful, imply a similar style of living. Advancing technologies and materials allows for a more experimental approach to combining aesthetics with usefulness. In any case, practical is certainly no longer a synonym for unsightly.

DECHEM STUDIO
Phenomena, 2017 / Bomma

Bomma, founded in 2012 to produce state-of-the-art lighting, is the newest brand among the Czech glass making community. Fusing centuries of glass making traditions in East Bohemia with ultra-modern technologies, the manufacturer has also initiated many interesting collaborations with talented designers. Not only does the highest quality matter, but so too does the aesthetic aspect, which is at the core of the brand's products. "Bomma produces 6 tons of refined, extra clear crystal each and every day. Our high-tech, bespoke machinery for precise melting and measuring allows our craftsmen to reach their maximum potential for manual finishing, enhancing what was always great and making it splendid", reads the statement by the team of 300 craftsmen. While glass is a challenging material, if manufactured skilfully, it can result in refined, unique objects. One of the most striking realizations in Bomma's portfolio is the *Phenomena* collection.

The inspiration for the collection was simple shapes such as circles, triangles, rectangles and ovals. This experiment with geometry is enhanced by a sophisticated play of colours. Each softly rounded shape is expressed in a different hue. The quality of the materials used and the uniqueness of the glassblowing process influences the palette's gradient. While the saturation of the colours differs, the light diffused by the glowing lamps creates a poetic atmosphere. The *Phenomena* collection, be it hung together as a group, or individually, magically transforms the space. "The term 'phenomenon' comes from the Greek word for 'appearance'. The forms are what you see on first sight." the designers explain. "In Plato's idealist philosophy, *phenomena* are transient, likenesses of the

eternal, perfect forms and so are not truly real." they add.

Prague-based DECHEM Studio was established by Michaela Tomišková and Jakub Janďourek in 2012. After studies at the Novy Bor School of Glass, Michaela Tomišková continued her education at the Academy of Arts in Prague. Jakub Janďourek worked for several acclaimed design studios in the lighting industry. The duo focuses on creating unique handmade glass objects and expertly merges the complex aspects of design and production. When working on light fixtures and lighting objects, DECHEM combines traditional production techniques and lyrical forms while placing a stress on grace and minimum shaping to allow "the specific optical colour qualities of the material to shine through".

NOÉ DUCHAUFOUR-LAWRANCE
Aqua Surfboard, 2018 / NDL Editions

"It takes knowledge, control and a good dose of instinct to ride waves. The control of water is also essential in watercolour techniques where fading looks so effortless and so poetic. *Aqua* is designed for the waves." This poetic description by one of the most outstanding French designers, Noé Duchaufour-Lawrance, characterizes his *Aqua* surfboard for NDL Editions. The board, an object which is not often picked by designers, gains here a sculptural quality. As with the designer's other works, this one shows his academic training in sculpture (followed however by a degree in furniture design from the prestigious Les Arts Décoratifs). "His sculptural work showcases a respect for the past, combined with a simplicity of line and an honest desire to create pieces that last." declares his statement. While working across a wide range of disciplines and materials, Duchaufour-Lawrance draws inspiration from nature. Whether he designs furniture, home accessories or interiors, the references to the organic world are strong and intricate. The designer's exceptional sense of observation is perfectly attuned to his ability to transpose the natural forms into objects for everyday use.

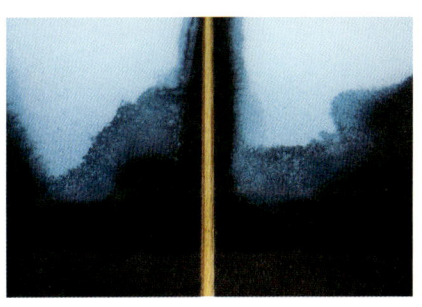

The *Aqua* surfboard, designed for interacting with waves, is fueled by the notion of nature. The glossy and distinctive surface of the board seems to echo the responsive movement of the water and the way it is filtered by the light. The remarkable colour effect, together with the softly rounded shapes, alludes more to a sea creature rather than a physical object, and thus harmonizes perfectly with water. The natural form meets the finest craftsmanship, resulting in a visually sensational surfboard. Duchaufour-Lawrance mastered the art of blending his designs smoothly with their surroundings, whatever that might be. "An object is naturally obliged to respond to a need, without creating others. From this absolute necessity, it must be a vehicle for meaning and emotions." he states, and he indeed approaches the design of every object individually. Forms and materials are used not to execute any universal style, but to find a perfect language that reflects the specific needs of each project.

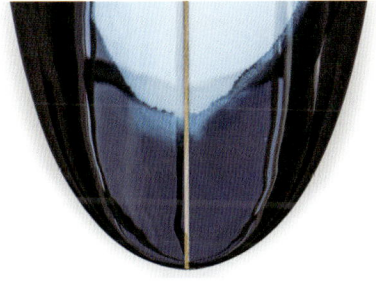

STUDIO ORIJEEN
Colour Flow, 2016

Seoul-based studio Orijeen, established by Jeen Seo in 2015, has been working on a wide range of projects in the fields of furniture, products, space and concept research design. The practice is focused on the relationship between humans, objects and the environment, and *Colour Flow* is their most spectacular and poetic project so far. The surface of the wardrobe is lenticular, which means that it can literally change its colour depending on the user's position or movement. But the piece is not merely colourful furniture, the interactive design actually needs the user to display its full, and extremely beautiful potential. Viewing the piece from various angles provides a rainbow of changing hues: the interior never looks the same. Like a chameleon, Orijeen's wardrobe features shades from yellow to blue. The designer's goal was to stress the relationship between us (the users) and the objects surrounding us, the ways in which we co-exist in our everyday lives.

"By changing colour depending on the user's position and movement, he or she is able to immediately realize the connection between them. This recognition might help people more actively and joyfully experience the objects, and communicate with them." muses Seo.

This magical effect is made possible by the ingenious use of a translucent plastic sheet, which is equipped with a set of small, convex lenses on one side, while the other side remains a flat surface. The lenses create the illusion of depth even though the surface is two-dimensional. Owners of this unusual piece of furniture see it with a different skin every time they move across the interior. It also gleams differently depending on the light entering the space. The unusual, curved shape of the wardrobe enhances the shimmering effect and makes the play of colours even more fascinating. With its curvaceous lines, one can admire the significant volume from various angles. The inside is made of wood. It looks like any other wardrobe, and can be used as such. The *Lenticular* Collection also includes an oval cabinet, with curves similar to those of the wardrobe. Based on four tiny legs, it glows with hues of red, violet and magenta, and creates an optically dazzling set.

MONICA FÖRSTER
Melange Lounge chair, 2018 / Wittmann

Monica Förster is one of the leading Swedish designers. Based in Stockholm, she collaborates with numerous brands around the world to design some exquisite pieces of furniture. Since 2015, the designer has also worked as a creative advisor for a number of design companies. A strong sense of form and a quest for the highest quality define Förster's style, which is also characterized by experimentation with both materials and technologies. The designer likes to blend modern looks with old craft techniques. "I sometimes say that I'm not interested in form, but that may not be entirely true. What I mean is simply that the idea behind each project is more important. When the idea is set I focus on shape, colour and detail." she comments.

Clear lines and a distinctive shape are the DNA of the *Melange lounge chair* designed for Wittmann. Förster's style is called by some, quite accurately, "a fusion of Viennese tradition with Scandinavian flair". The soft, curvaceous seat, and the separate, velvet-soft leather backrest offer ideal comfort and true relaxation.

Well-thought-out, down to the tiniest detail, it shows Förster's natural sense of form and materials. *Melange's* leather back and cushions are available in numerous colour options, either monochromatic or contrasting. Compared to the seating elements, the chair's structure looks very light and comes in both wooden and metallic variants. The wooden version creates a cosier impression, while the metallic one appears as if the comfortable seat was floating above the ground. The lounge chair is part of a small collection, which also features a sofa and three tables: Bridge Table, Stool Table and Handle Table. All of the items are independent from each other, yet are complementary when arranged next to one another. "In the tradition of Josef Frank and free of any dogma, the *Melange* collection strikes the perfect balance between tradition and modernity, hand craftsmanship and precision engineering." boasts the manufacturer. Förster created the collection with small spaces and the contemporary, nomadic lifestyle in mind. The lounge chair is the strongest piece of the collection and it is simply beautiful.

PATRICIA URQUIOLA AND FEDERICO PEPE
Credenza, 2016 / Editions Milano

Born in Spain and based in Milan, Patricia Urquiola is an architect by education. After working with designers like Achille Castiglioni and Vico Magistretti, she established her own studio in 2001. While collaborating with a large number of international companies, she has also been Cassina's Art Director since 2015. The practice of this internationally celebrated designer focuses on product design, architecture and installations in a truly wide range of projects. Federico Pepe is an artist, graphic designer, video-maker and typographer. "I started my career doing advertising. Not long after, I realized that commissioned works did not give me the opportunity to express everything that I wanted to express and do everything that I wanted to do." he explains about his multifaceted creative activity. Apart from collaborating with celebrated artists like Maurizio Catellan or Pierpaolo Ferrari, Pepe founded the art magazine *Le Dictateur*.

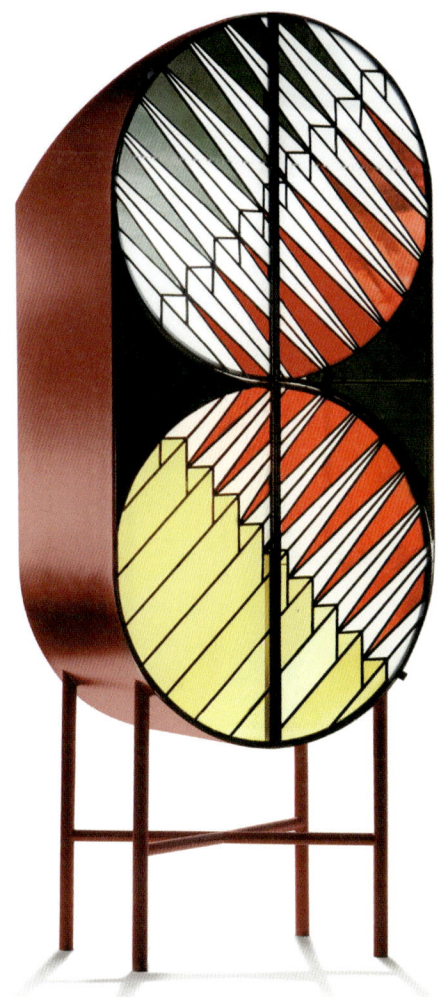

Urquiola and Pepe teamed up to design these exquisite cabinets ("credenza" in Italian, which also means "faith/belief") drawing inspiration from stained glass church windows. Urquiola was inspired by the windows of holy sites such as those created by Gerhard Richter at Cologne Cathedral. The result of this unique collaboration between the duo and the manufacturer is a very successful fusion of centuries-old lead-glass craftsmanship and contemporary patterns crafted by Italian craftsmen. The light passing through the coloured glass is at the core of both models, vertical and horizontal. The patterns, which are a variation on geometric shapes, display Pepe's graphic skills, and remind one of a kaleidoscope. The spectacular interplay of triangles, circles and rectangles is enhanced by the selection of colours. Thanks to invisible joints, the cabinet's doors open easily without disrupting the geometric design. To focus attention on the dazzling stained-glass panels, they are installed on simple yet unconventional oval structures. *Credenza* is a sophisticated combination of original forms and refined colours. In addition to the cabinets, which are manufactured as a limited edition. The *Credenza* collection also features a room divider, which uses the same multicoloured stained-glass technique.

TOMÁS ALONSO
Prism Bowl, 2016 /
Atelier Swarovski Home

Atelier Swarovski has been always proud of itself for its ground-breaking partnerships with renowned designers. Together, they push the boundaries of the material to dramatic effect. Working with crystal has never resulted in such fascinating objects as the Atelier's portfolio has done. One of the guest designers is a cosmopolitan talent, Tomás Alonso, who created a series of crystal and marble prisms made into sensational trays, vases and centrepieces as featured here. "These crystal objects are like jewellery for the home." says the designer. Indeed, the brightly coloured crystal combined with noble marble creates an exceptionally classy idea for interior decor. Alonso aimed at creating a stunning colour effect, which he achieved by using precisely cut angles of the multicoloured crystal prisms that are bound with marble bases. The visual effect is both glamorous and mystifying. As the user moves, looking at these unique objects from various angles, a beautiful spectacle of shadows and hues is initiated, as the crystal interacts with the rays of light.

The way we coexist with objects around us and how we establish the relationship with them are the recurrent themes in Alonso's work. The reflective crystal prisms with their jewel-like glazes are enhanced by the designer's signature vivid colour play. The faceted Swarovski crystals radiate varying and contrasting colour tones to boost the decorative aspect of a perfectly practical everyday object. As with Alonso's other designs, the centrepiece also exemplifies an elegant functionality. The complex structure of the fragile crystal body is contrastingly merged with the smooth and solid marble, which is a very original concept. "I experiment with structures, proportions and spatial relationships to create objects that offer something new, but maintaining a strong relationship with their use and context." as Alonso explains his vision.

Born in Spain, Alonso set out on an inspirational journey at the age of 19. After living, studying and developing a professional practice in the USA, Italy and Australia, the designer finally moved to London, where he is now based, to complete an MA at the Royal College of Art. 2006 marked the co-founding of the design collective OKAY studio. Alonso works on furniture, product, lighting and both interior and exhibition design, exploring the expressive potential of each specific material. His designs are elegant, expressive and yet focused on practical solutions.

FRONT
Water Steps, 2016 / Axor

FRONT was among the designers and architects invited by the bathroom brand Axor, in 2016, to create a range of original faucets. Axor is famous for challenging traditional solutions and for innovating together with the leading masters of design today, which was also at the core of the *WaterDream* project. The designers were given complete creative freedom to develop innovative mixer spouts. The brand only encouraged them to experiment with forms and materials in order to define the "significance and value of water within our living environment". Testing the boundaries of customization was another goal of the brand. Next to David Adjaye, Werner Aisslinger, GamFratesi and Jean-Marie Massaud, Axor also invited the Swedish designer duo FRONT to create their own spout.

  For Sofia Lagerkvist and Anna Lindgren, who established their Stockholm-based studio, it was the second collaboration with Axor, as they previously created a shower installation made from a maze of copper pipes. This time, as Lagerkvist recollects: "They said 'you can rethink what a tap can be', which was music to our ears as designers." The duo's response was a beautiful, sculptural spout made of metal. As the focus was on the playful exchange between form and water, their solution consists of two conical bowls displaying the flow of water, which also becomes a decorative element. One of the vessels is gracefully suspended in the air, which adds lightness to this exquisite structure. Additionally, the stream tumbling through these unusually shaped steps resembles a natural waterfall and the visual effect is stunning. "It aesthetically and acoustically underlines the emotional potential of the natural element as it flows over PVD-finished, metallic surfaces." state the designers. "We like the idea of working with sound because it's not something designers usually think about." they added. FRONT, well-known for their ingenious ideas and unconventional experiments with both forms and materials, transformed the everyday practice of using a tap into a multi-sensory experience, which may be connected with the duo's passion for magic. Axor previously collaborated with designers like Nendo (which resulted in a surreal installation merging showers with a series of lamps) and Philippe Starck (who created an innovative water-saving tap).

FORMAFANTASMA
Pigmento storage box, 2018 /
Nude Glass

Amsterdam-based Studio Formafantasma was founded by an Italian designer duo. Andrea Trimarchi and Simone Farresin graduated from the Design Academy in Eindhoven in 2009 and immediately started pursuing their professional careers as designers. Experimentation with materials or exploration of the relationship between tradition and local culture are characteristic elements of their practice. "Whether designing for a client or investigating alternative applications of materials, Studio Formafantasma applies the same rigorous attention to context, process and detail to every project they undertake." they state.

For the Istanbul-based design brand Nude, the duo designed a storage box as part of a tableware collection. Their expertly crafted *Pigmento* draws from the tradition of the mouth-blown technique and celebrates artisan craftsmanship. The opaque glass of this short, cylindrical container with a lid is decorated with flashes of coloured pigment. While the storage box has a beige accent on the flat-domed lid, the frosted surfaces of other objects in the *Pigmento* glassware collection are embellished with powder rose, yellow or grey hues. In all the variants, the pastel colour combinations work well with the milky structure of the glass. The visual effect is ephemeral and romantic. Both the palette and the colour application remind us of tender flower petals. As in all of the pieces from the *Pigmento* series, the container also delights the eye with a great sense of form.

By rounding the edges, the designers achieved a delicacy that fits perfectly into a cozy interior. At the same time, the simple shapes ideally define the item's functional role. As the collection is handmade, each piece differs and is thus unique. Additionally, the flashes of colour create various imaginative motifs. The *Pigmento* storage box is an alluring decorative statement matching the manufacturer's portfolio. Nude creates contemporary glassware made of lead-free crystal glass in the spirit of simplicity. Apart from experimenting with unusual materials (like lava, beetle shells or pastry), Formafantasma is also known for exploring colour effects. Another of their delightful realizations was the *Cromatica* collection for the Italian ceramics brand CEDIT Ceramiche d'Italia. The duo also designed tiles, which can render shadow effects onto surfaces, inspired by the colour range once used by architect and designer Ettore Sottsass.

NERI & HU
Ren Magazine Rack, 2016 / Poltrona Frau

The *Ren* is a sophisticated collection of accessories dedicated to storage. A result of studies of the home entryway by Chinese designer duo Neri&Hu, it features "a series of objects that are hybrid in their function and materials", as described by Poltrona Frau, the manufacturer. All elements of the collection can be used in various spaces and arranged in different combinations. It initially comprised a freestanding mirror coat rack, a small table, a console table, a wall-mounted mirror coat rack and valet stand, later expanding to include a bookcase, a table mirror and the magazine rack presented here. The designers call these objects "supporting actors" for the main furniture-characters of the household, like sofas, beds or tables. The name of the collection originates from the Chinese ideogram"人"(ren), which means "a person" and has a two-stroke pictographic representation referring to the human figure. While one of the strokes is slightly longer, both depend on each other for stability. Accordingly, Neri&Hu based the collection's structures on simple lines supported by two elements referring to the shape of "人". As with other pieces in the series, the frame of the rack is made of solid Canaletto walnut. It holds a sheet of Cuoio Saddle Extra leather, which is attached to the upper wooden crosspiece by two brushed steel bars with a matt brass finish. The latter detail adds a sophisticated touch. This elegant container for magazines, executed with great attention to detail, is a balancing act. The structure referring to the Chinese ideogram "人" is particularly highlighted in this piece as it carries a U-shaped shelf to hold the magazines. Suspended in the air, it looks light and harmonious.

Neri&Hu was established in 2004 by Lyndon Neri and Rossana Hu as an interdisciplinary architectural design practice and has headquarters in Shanghai and an office in London. The studio's projects range from architecture, interior and master planning to graphic and product design. With a strong stress on research, the duo "desires to anchor its work on the dynamic interaction of experience, detail, material, form, and light rather than conforming to a formulaic style. The ultimate significance behind each project comes from how the built forms create meaning through their physical representations", they state.

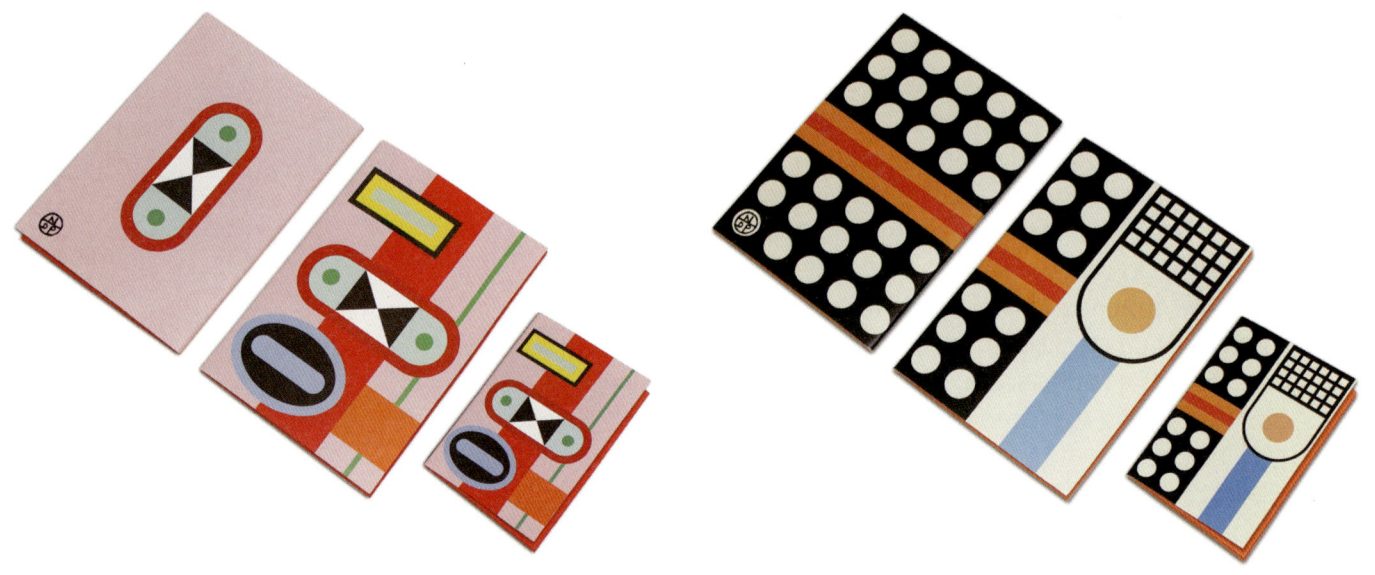

NATHALIE DU PASQUIER
Notebooks' covers, 2016 / Rubberband

The designer's official biography reads: "Nathalie Du Pasquier was born in Bordeaux (France) in 1957, she has lived in Milano since 1979. Until 1986 she worked as a designer and was a founder member of Memphis. She designed numerous 'decorated surfaces': textiles, carpets, plastic laminates, and some furniture and objects. In 1987, painting became her main activity." Nevertheless, Du Pasquier collaborated in 2016 with the Mumbai-based label Rubberband, which offers a wide variety of stationery goods, including a collection co-created with artists. The philosophy behind their notebooks, journals, notepads, planners as well as memo pads and pens, is simple and functional design with a strong sense of style. Another feature that characterizes their designs is the use of vivid colours. Founded in 2007 by Ajay Shah, the brand also introduced a collection of furniture.

Du Pasquier's design for Rubberband's Artist Collection includes covers of a series of six notebooks in two sizes (designed by Shah, they are available in A5

and A6). Each vibrates with a totally different pattern, which continues on both the front and the back covers. Drawing inspiration from the Memphis aesthetics, the design of the notebooks uses geometry and vivid colours in inventive sequences. The designer's sense of form and colour results in playful and intriguing arrangements. Blocky shapes as well as strong contrasts of vivid colours turn the notebooks into artistic yet very practical objects of desire. Some visual motifs use optical illusion to trick our eyes, others delight with the interplay of geometric shapes. The colour of the pages is, in each case, adjusted to reflect the palette of the cover composition.

    Du Pasquier's collection is fun, loud and must-have stationery to stimulate the senses. These state-of-the-art design notebooks translate the Memphis visual language, which is very popular again today. "It was probably the beginning of a new era." says Du Pasquier about the group's beginnings. "Form did not have to follow function any more, and design was about communication." she adds. Interestingly, in the wake of the Memphis revival, Du Pasquier has collaborated with several brands. Her compelling patterns were applied to cushions, rugs and accessories as well as garments.

#4

GOOD DESIGN MAKES
A PRODUCT UNDERSTANDABLE

"It clarifies the product's
structure. Better still, it
can make the product talk.
At best, it is self-explanatory."

Dieter Rams

The user should understand from the very first moment the story behind a design — what it is for and how to use it. Even if that sounds obvious, it is often not so easy to achieve. Some designers push the boundaries of the aesthetic side so far that the result is completely obscure, even if visually intriguing. The product should speak clearly and understandably. Its structure and function should not require any additional explanation, even when it is meant to please the eye. Our interaction with products should be intuitive and natural, otherwise their role in our lives is not satisfactory enough. Design is meant to improve life and not to complicate it. Hence, designers have a difficult task to fuse their own unique vision with how it might be interpreted by the user. Translating an original idea into a perfectly functional and eye-pleasing object is at stake here.

CONSTANCE GUISSET
Fusca, 2018 / Bosa

Constance Guisset founded her studio in 2009 to work on product and interior design as well as on scenography. The main goal of her team of designers and architects is to create "light and animated objects, aiming to arouse wonder and to invoke a moment of escaping into dreams". Guisset does not look for extraordinary objects; her portfolio consists of lamps, mirrors and furniture. However, the way the designer interprets each object is highly original and breathes fresh air into the way we perceive traditional objects in our surroundings. This applies to the *Fusca* vase, designed for the Italian manufacturer Bosa. This ceramic vase is characterised by its beautifully voluptuous and curious form. Quite unusually for a vase, its body is not the most important part of its composition.

Opening like a handheld fan, the collar's expansive surface is covered with rhythmic texture. The evocative shape of the vase, which is available in a wide range of colours and finishes, brings many associations to mind. The most obvious one is connected with the natural world, and suggest the leaf of a waterlily's or a lion's mane. The regularly applied decoration enhances the organic character of the shape and subtly suggests movement, as if imitating an opening flower, which perfectly echoes the vase's function. Guisset's unorthodox approach to vase design makes it not only eye-catching, but also practical. The spread collar will enhance flower arrangements by serving as a screen-like support. *Fusca* acts as an elegant ceramic wrapping for any bouquet. The designer often plays with the materials to create an impression of movement. For example, in her iconic *Drapée* chair steel rods are bent to form curving lines resembling fabric draped over the backrest and the seat.

    Fusca's manufacturer, Bosa, is proud of itself in its long traditions (Italo Bosa initiated ceramic production in 1976) and of applying ancient techniques to producing handmade objects. A rich colour palette and precious finishes are characteristics of Bosa's ceramic products. In collaboration with leading designers, the brand continues its research and innovative experiments to "transform formal and functional conventions into new interpretations, new functions and fantastic worlds".

CHRISTIAN WERNER
Lilu, 2018 / Interlübke

Lilu is the result of the partnership between German industrial designer, Christian Werner, and manufacturer Interlübke. This unique shelving system combines an individual panel design and a storage space. It is much more than a conventional shelf and delights the user with its countless possibilities for arranging the elements. Each setting can create a totally different visual effect on the wall. Available in three sizes, with various thicknesses, different shelf depths and variable heights of the back, the system can be adjusted to the objects the user plans to display, and to the interior's character. Werner's shelving system can also be equipped with an attractive backlight, featuring dimming and colour temperature control, designed to create an impression that the shelf is floating freely in space. In terms of colour, the collection has been well thought through to allow for harmonic compositions whatever shelf combinations the users decide to create. The wide range of hues allows multiple possible arrangements.

On its own, above or adjacent to the sideboard, horizontal or vertical, *Lilu* encourages personalised design, which can be re-arranged whenever the user wishes. The shelves can be easily moved around by hand. The shelf's L-shape forms a perfect stage-like space to store and display various items and decorations. Lightness and elegance define this extremely flexible concept. The system is a perfect demonstration of the brand's philosophy: First of all, freedom, which is understood as the ability to provide users with the maximum of individuality and flexibility of their furniture; secondly, encouraging users to create minimalist designs. "That is how classics are born." reads the statement; and finally, joy that Interlübke's furniture gives to its users. *Lilu* not only matches the rest of the manufacturer's collections, but also works well in any interior, be it a kitchen, a living room, or an entrance hall.

Christian Werner is an established designer based in the German city of Hollenstedt. He specializes in furniture design, which he has developed over the last 25 years. The designer collaborates with a number of leading European manufacturers, aiming at creating timeless pieces. While bare shapes and simplicity are Werner's signature formal language, forms and materials should be, according to the designer, the expression of emotions and sensuality.

SOU FUJIMOTO
The Smallest Library/Bookchair, 2017 /
Alias

    Acclaimed Japanese architect, Sou Fujimoto, is known for exploring the relationship between architectural space and the human body in his works. In the wake of this study, he invented an innovative piece of furniture; an amalgam of a typical bookcase plus a built-in chair, which forms part of the main structure. In order to be used, the chair slots in and out of the bookcase. While allowing the user's body to rest, it also contains shelves for storage. In the compact position, with the seat nested in the bookcase, the layout of the shelves is nearly unaltered. However, thanks to the sinusoid profile (the seat and back are formed from a single piece of wood), the chair-element is visible and the way it functions made obvious. "*Bookchair* comes to life through the aggregation of a new element, the chair within the bookcase, based on a concept that aims to reflect the basic, fundamental relationship between a book and its reader." explains Fujimoto.

Extracting the chair requires action from the user. The full potential of the design is thus gained by interaction. *Bookchair* is a perfect solution for all booklovers who live in a small space. Providing with both a bookcase to store books and a seat for enjoying reading is very practical as it takes up less space with no need for additional pieces of furniture. Moreover, home libraries often dominate the space by being massive, while Fujimoto's structure is light and semi-transparent. The main focus is on the display of books with the shelves reduced to a strict minimum. The design also exemplifies the values of the producer — technological lightness, versatility and innovation. Since 1976, the Italian brand Alias has collaborated on their collections with numerous renowned designers. Made of wooden fibre panels, the *Bookchair* reflects the manufacturer's eco-design objective.

Fujimoto graduated in architecture from the Faculty of Engineering at Tokyo University. His realizations are continual attempts to redefine space. The architect's distinctive style is characterized by light and spatial, yet minimalist, constructions employing geometry. Whether applied to buildings or objects, Fujimoto's approach is fresh and innovative. The results, often inspired by nature, are visually stunning, like a transparent house, a cloud pavilion, or a tree-inspired apartment building to name but a few.

CECILIE MANZ
COMPILE Bookends, 2016 / Muuto

"*COMPILE* bookends add a sculptural feature to your shelving system, with clear lines and multiple display options for your favourite books and magazines." as Cecilie Manz describes the concept. "The bookend supports itself, ensuring unrestricted movement and creative freedom of use. It serves as a functional element, adding colour and character to shelves at home or in the office." she adds. What strikes one first about this original collection of bookends is their minimalist look and versatility. While the forms have been reduced to their essentials, the various heights provide flexibility, which is important for storing books. It is rare for anyone to own books of only one size. Our libraries are usually much more diverse, and Manz's design accommodates various needs. Thanks to the proportions of this book support system, it can be placed in numerous positions, adding visual variety to the shelves' look.

Their geometric forms and their functional simplicity make the bookends perfect for using in any interior, regardless of the space's design or role. Crafted with precision, the *COMPILE* series is made of laser-cut steel sheets and bent into shape with softly curved corners. The bookends are coated with high-quality powder in three colours that harmonize with each other: green-beige, grey and plum. In addition to fulfilling their practical function, the pure silhouettes of *COMPILE* bookends provide an elegant and sculptural decorative

element for the shelves. Manz's sense of material and form is evident and draws from Nordic aesthetics. "There are skilled craftsmen all over the world, but what makes Scandinavian design successful is our feel for materials and attention to detail." the designer claims, "Scandinavian design is minimalist and humble with great respect for each single material."

Cecilie Manz, one of the prominent stars of the Danish and international design community today, creates furniture, glass, lamps, and ceramics. She established her Copenhagen-based studio in 1998 after graduation from The Royal Danish Academy of Fine Arts, The School of Design, and the University of Art and Design in Helsinki. As she states, she designs things that have meaning to her. Function is essential to Manz. However, she stresses the importance of having a clear and good reason that legitimizes designing a new object.

TOMAS KRAL
Parrot, 2017 / Nude Glass

The bird-shaped silhouette of this unique carafe is part of its practical aspect, and even enhances it. Slovakian-born designer, Tomas Kral, whose studio is based in Switzerland, wanted to put a smile on the user's face, but the result actually brought additional functionality. The designer's playful idea is executed in a refined way. *Parrot* is a combination of hand-blown glass and hand decoration, which makes the object both beautiful and precious. Decoration empowers its functionality. Handmade and hand-painted vertical cuts etched on the body, reminiscent of feathers, prevent the hand from slipping when pouring water. A similar motif, increasing one's grip, appears on the glass accompanying the carafe. Etching in glass also introduces an interesting play of reflections, particularly when the *Parrot* or the tumbler is filled with water.

Just as we associate the bird with exotic climates, we tend to use the carafe when it's hot. Hence the sun's rays can animate the object's body beautifully. Its protruding metal sprout resembles the bird's beak and allows for an elegant, and efficient flow of water. These two details — the beak and the cuts, create the magic in this otherwise very clear and minimalistic silhouette. "I wanted to create something that would remind people of something they can't quite put their finger on, whilst being modern." comments Kral. His exotic set of a carafe with a tumbler is available in three colours. Easy to use and practical, this award-winning set is simply stunning. The designer's reinterpretation of a traditional carafe is humorous and aesthetically sophisticated. As such the *Parrot* is an exquisite decoration to land on our tables.

Kral had a degree of the École cantonale d'art de Lausanne (Ecal), and established his own practice in the city back in 2008. Kral's approach to design prioritizes preoccupation for materials and processes, regardless if the designer works in glass, cork or ceramic. The wide range of projects spanning from lighting and furniture to accessories is fueled by both tradition and everyday situations, which Kral translates into objects with a great sense of humour and fantasy. The designer's objective is to find new creative approaches, innovative shapes, intriguing details, while also experimenting with craftsmanship.

GUILLAUME DELVIGNE
Horizon Collection, 2016 /
Cristal de Sèvres

Cristal de Sèvres is a manufacturer with a long history and great traditions. It was established in 1750 at the initiative of Madame de Pompadour, who wanted to "create simple and elegant collections, objects of desire and exclusivity". The quality of the manufacturer's luxury glassware is remarkable and its refined style is recognizable. While keeping a centuries-old tradition alive by creating timeless designs, the company regularly reinvigorates its portfolio by working with leading designers to mirror the aesthetics of the time. One of the latest examples of adding this contemporary touch is Guillaume Delvigne's *Horizon* collection. Contacted by Hélène Triboulet, who at the time had just become the brand's artistic director, the designer was invited to participate in revitalizing their style.

The key word for the commission was "After work" and they were seeking a complete range of glasses for bars. This elegant selection of 11 glasses for various alcoholic drinks, among them wine, champagne, whisky, vodka or cocktails, is characterized by purity of crystal and timeless shape. The silhouette of each glass matches the character of specific alcohol to enhance their degustation and is perfectly recognizable. One of the challenges the designer had to face was to link the pieces visually with each other despite the variety of shapes, and to achieve a consistent style. "To make the collection legible and coherent, I tried to rationalize certain heights and diameters to obtain a maximum of common elements.

The outlines of the glasses come from very pure and tense geometric shapes, a language that I develop throughout my work." explains Delvigne. "This desire caused a small technical challenge because this rigor of lines is not obvious to be transposed into the glass." the designer admits.

The shapes of the bowls are subtly rounded and the stems are elegantly prolonged, which, together with the precision of lines and robust bases, displays a beautiful balance harmoniously expressed in glass. Delvigne's sense of geometry and proportions contribute to a contemporary look, which is timeless at the same time. His collection has an air of class and sophistication. In addition to the glassware, the *Horizon* collection includes a carafe and an ice bucket. Delvigne studied at the École de Design Nantes Atlantique and at the Politecnico di Milano. After working alongside the renowned designers in Milan and Paris, he established his own studio in 2011. He has also been a member of the design collective Dito since 2006.

EMANUELE MAGINI
Blow Daybed, 2015 / Gufram

This unusual design does not come as a surprise to anyone knowing that the Italian designer, Emanuele Magini, graduated from Milan Politecnico with a final dissertation on the semiotics of holidays. Running his own studio since 2010, the designer has been famous for playful and innovatively interpreted objects. The *Blow* daybed statement reads: "It could be the perfect pop lounge chaise for your situational shrink. And maybe it might even work to help you overcome the fear of water. In its features, we can clearly see the reference to the air mattress of the seventies, as well as its ironic charge. Comfortable and playful, *Blow* takes idleness to extremes. With sunglasses and a cocktail in your hand, no wave can hurt you, nor can the sun burn you." The imitation of an inflatable mattress, which is strongly associated with a swimming pool, summer, sun and holidays, definitely sparks the imagination. And so the form of this daybed is a perfect allusion, and an encouragement. One can use it according to the joyful images it brings to mind.

Independent of the place or time of the year, Magini's design transports us to the world of leisure, and laziness. The designer makes perfect use of the evocative form and the emotions, in this case very positive, it invokes. He actually drew on his own holiday experiences, when the view of an air mattress left on a bench next to the beach caught his attention. Users get an ideal invitation for relaxation, which also emphasizes a daybed's main function. They can feel as if they were floating on a swimming pool. To provide comfort and to recreate the playful appeal, the daybed is cushioned with polyurethane foam, which is ribbed to imitate pockets of air and lined with a sustainable fabric from Danish textile brand Kvadrat. The top end has been angled upward to support the head and the structure elevated on four tubular aluminium legs.

The manufacturer, iconic brand Gufram, is quintessentially Italian. Founded in 1966, it has produced many fanciful, original and ironic objects, like lips-shaped sofas, cactus coat-stands or grass-like seats, in collaboration with top designers.

MICHAEL SODEAU
Anything Collection, 2008 / HAY

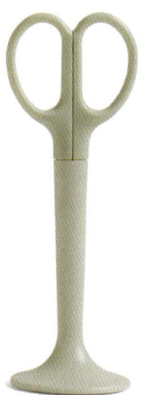

London-based Michael Sodeau, a graduate in product design from Central Saint Martin's College of Art & Design, runs a multidisciplinary studio and works across various design fields. His philosophy is embodied in simple solutions and problem solving, which he realizes by designing pieces of furniture distinctive in style, lighting and accessories. The designer's ideas are truly original visions of everyday objects. Creative thinking, an unorthodox approach to the forms, as well as exploration of a variety of materials leads to imaginative objects. Their innovativeness is not limited to their fresh looks. In Sodeau's designs, form is followed by functionality. Whether it is a coffee maker and mug set, a letter opener or coat hooks, we can be sure that the objects' curious shapes only enhance their practical aspect. "You try to build stories around products. You think about how people are going to interact with them, where they're going to be seen, how other products will associate with them. That's how it evolves." the designer says.

Anything collection was designed for HAY, the famous Danish brand that makes good design available to a large audience. "Hay's continued vision is to create straightforward, functional and aesthetic design in cooperation with some of the world's most talented, curious and courageous designers." states the brand as its main mission. In line with this spirit, Sodeau's collection of office essentials is not just another desk set. The compact forms hidden in plastic casting are somehow a remedy for the boredom office work can sometimes create. They enable their users to enjoy desk-work again. The stapler, easy to grasp quickly in one hand, is quite massive in shape to help add pressure when stapling documents.

The tape is placed on an unusually high dispenser, which is stable enough to allow cutting off the required piece of tape using only one hand. The scissors, hidden in a fitting and well balanced stand, are ready for action with just an effortless lift. The collection is available in three muted hues (green, yellow and beige). It will be a simple and chic visual accent for any desk, and a precious support in performing office tasks.

SHANE SCHNECK
Dish Drainer, 2017 / HAY

      This is another design for HAY, the design brand founded by Rolf and Mette Hay in 2002: a playful dishwashing set, which resembles an intriguing landscape rather than kitchen equipment. Designed by Shane Schneck, who is a prolific contributor to the Danish brand's portfolio, this functional solution for draining the dishes consists of three components: a ridged melamine tray, a steel plate rack, and a silicone cutlery holder. However, each element is separate and can be freely arranged according to the user's needs. How the designer plays with contrasting shapes, materials and colours seems the most refreshing aspect of the set. The combination of ribbed texture for the flat, extensive base with the tubular structure of the rack and the curvaceous flat surface of the cutlery holder is imaginative and works well. This diversity adds a touch of class to the sink, and a pinch of originality to the kitchen equipment. Utensils designed to drain dishes are usually regarded as purely practical objects. Schneck's set is also perfectly functional

and makes washing dishes an easier and more pleasant task. Thanks to these inventive tools, it will be also done properly. The tray is made to allow water to drain away and can also accommodate several racks (each has slots for 8 plates). At the same time, the designer shows that even such a down-to-earth object can become a well-designed kitchen accessory. The graphic touch of Scandinavian design and the sophisticated hues make it fun not to have a dishwasher.

Schneck is an American designer living and working in Sweden. After studying Architecture at Miami University in Oxford, Ohio, and working with Piero Lissoni as Senior Industrial Designer at the Lissoni Associati in Milan, he founded his Stockholm-based Office for Design Studio in 2010. His philosophy in his own words: "my design ethos is to create simple yet innovative products that challenge industry standards." Another common feature is providing as much flexibility as possible and furnishing users with designs that allow numerous configuration possibilities (one of his designs is a lamp which can be used in four different positions). Schneck's designs often comprise an element of surprise, are unusual, and quintessentially playful.

CLARA VON ZWEIGBERGK
Candle Holder, 2017 / HAY + IKEA

In 2017, IKEA and HAY teamed up to create a range of over 30 pieces of furniture and homeware products under the name of *Ypperling* collection. "We learned a lot of things from this collaboration that we can apply to our own company: the simplicity in the IKEA supply chain, and making something that's complex simpler, and therefore better and less expensive." said Rolf Hay, the co-founder of HAY. One of the collection's elements was the *Candle Holder* designed by Clara von Zweigbergk. The Stockholm-based designer graduated from Beckmans School of Design in her home city and continued her education at Art Center College of Design in Pasadena, California. She co-founded and was a partner in a multidisciplinary design studio Rivieran. Von Zweigbergk also worked as a senior graphic designer at Lissoni Associati in Milan.

Upon her return to Stockholm, she established her own design studio "pursuing a great interest in paper, colour, typography and form". Her practice is dominated by visual identities, photo art direction and a series of products. Since 2010 Von Zweigbergk has closely collaborated with HAY on designing homeware objects and developing their visual identity (including their catalogues). The designer however, designs products for other international brands. Simple and well-balanced lines, and a great sense of colour, are the designer's signature touches.

Within the *Ypperling* collection, Von Zweigbergk designed a candle-holder in cast alloy. The idea is simple and evocative, as the designer mimics the form of melted wax in circular terrace-like layers. With its rhythmic base, it harmonizes nicely with the surroundings wherever it may be displayed. Meant for a single slim candle, the design refers to the most basic candles used in households before the invention of electricity. However, it is not designed to be carried around, but only to be used in a fixed position. To make the object safe, a soft slide protector underneath the base keeps the candle-holder firmly in place and spares the surface below. Available in several colours through IKEA, it is an inexpensive and well-designed decorative object.

#5

GOOD DESIGN IS UNOBTRUSIVE

"Products that fulfil a purpose are like tools. They are neither decorative objects nor works of art. Their design should, therefore, be both neutral and restrained to leave room for the user's self-expression."

Dieter Rams

In an age of overproduction, designs desperately try to catch our attention. Far too often, and quite wrongly, we tend to treat objects as status symbols prioritizing their visual aspect. The flashier they are, the better. Rams advocates a more reasonable attitude: "We must drastically reduce the chaos of shapes, colours, and symbols that surround us." he states, "We need to defend ourselves against being overwhelmed with stimuli and return to the pure and simple in order to reclaim some leeway for our own selves." Even if aesthetically pleasant, products are tools that we use to fulfil certain purposes, and to make our lives easier and better. They should, therefore, be elements of the bigger picture, without dominating it. They should contribute to reflecting the user's taste and style of life in an inconspicuous way.

ANDERSSEN & VOLL
Five Pouf, 2016 / Muuto

"Crafted with precision" is the motto of the collection of these five-sided poufs designed by Anderssen & Voll for Muuto. The Norwegian designers teamed up with the Danish manufacturer, and the effect is quintessentially Scandinavian. The pentagon shape is emphasized by linear details, which looks very intriguing in combination with the softly rounded edges. The rhythmical ridged texture reminds the user of the earth's patterns seen from a bird's perspective. Five wedge-shaped sections embrace the pouf's shape and meet in the very middle of the top, creating a dynamic effect. "The design process was very much about tailoring; the quilted ribs are seemingly wrapped around the shape and enhance the dynamics of the pentagon." said Anderssen & Voll. The design is executed with an eye for detail.

While the wood fibre and plastic blend inject into the mould form the shell, the shell itself is upholstered with foam and fabric, which is glued and stapled using piping on the edges. A finishing touch, the swivel foot,

is of one-piece die cast aluminium. *Five Pouf* comes in four different muted colours (blue, grey, black and pink), which can also be arranged together in interesting combinations. The object works perfectly as additional seating or as a place where users can pile magazines, a blanket or rest their feet. The design is simple, practical and comfortable. It looks classy in the space, but at the same time its form does not scream at you.

Torbjørn Anderssen and Espen Voll established their common practice in Oslo in 2009 and were soon seen as one of the best Scandinavian design teams. The duo's studio explores various fields of design. However, the emphasis is clearly put on domestic objects. "A good product builds and expands on tradition while simultaneously breaking the rules of said tradition." they say provocatively, and accordingly they create objects with both a Nordic flair and a twist. Their design philosophy reads: "Modifications and elements of surprise, even changes that are less radical stimulate the thought and reflection of those who may not hold a particular interest in design. This tiny second of reflection is the window of opportunity where we can communicate with the users and that's what we strive to tap into."

INGA SEMPÉ
Ruban Mirror Collection, 2015 / Hay

The contrasting juxtaposition of a ribbon and mirror glass defines Inga Sempé's collection for HAY. The designer was interested in finding a solution to invent a light, but at the same time not raw, glass mirror. Here rectangular and square mirrors in five different formats have oak frames, which the designer decided to wrap with colourful textured ribbons. Each shape receives a different vibrant hue. The colours as well as the contrast between the tactile structure of the ribbon and the smooth surface of the mirror make an interesting visual statement. The sophisticated finish was meant to soften the edges, but also to function as a hook for hanging it. The latter function was created by adding a second piece of ribbon, attached with brass screws. "Framing a mirror sounds easy but to keep the initial light and graphic effect has been a long and complicated process." admits the designer. She also acknowledges that each element has been changed in the course of making, be it the way the ribbon was glued or the fixing system, to reduce the technical details to a necessary minimum and create a simple and affordable object. "I am interested in simplicity enhanced by a little more, hard to define, but that would make the difference with the existing objects." said the designer. The unusual formats of the mirrors drawn from various sources like mirrors that hung in old trains. The *Ruban* collection not only allows various original arrangements, individually or in a cluster, but also fits a range of interiors. The ribbon-edged mirrors are like framed pictures on the wall, only with a changing image.

Paris-based Sempé is one of the leading French designers. She graduated from the École Nationale Superieure de Création Industrielle (ENSCI) in Paris. After a one-year scholarship at the Villa Medici, Académie de France in Rome, she opened her own studio back in 2001. Sempé, assisted by two other designers, collaborates with Italian, French and Scandinavian manufacturers. Praised for the strong personality and the tactile nature of her work, the designer's explorations between materials and forms lead to distinctive interpretations of everyday objects.

KONSTANTIN GRCIC
Keyboard, 2014 / Marsotto Edizioni

Trained as a cabinet-maker at The John Makepeace School (Dorset, England), German designer Konstantin Grcic graduated in design from the Royal College of Art in London. The designer set up his studio, Konstantin Grcic Industrial Design (KGID) in Munich in 1991. His practice spans from developing furniture, lighting, visual branding or bathroom utensils to fashion accessories and a watch. As the statement reads, "Konstantin Grcic defines function in human terms, combining formal strictness with considerable mental acuity and humour. Each of his products is characterized by careful research into the history of design and architecture and his passion for technology and materials. Known for pared-down pieces, Grcic is often called a minimalist, but the designer himself prefers to speak of simplicity."

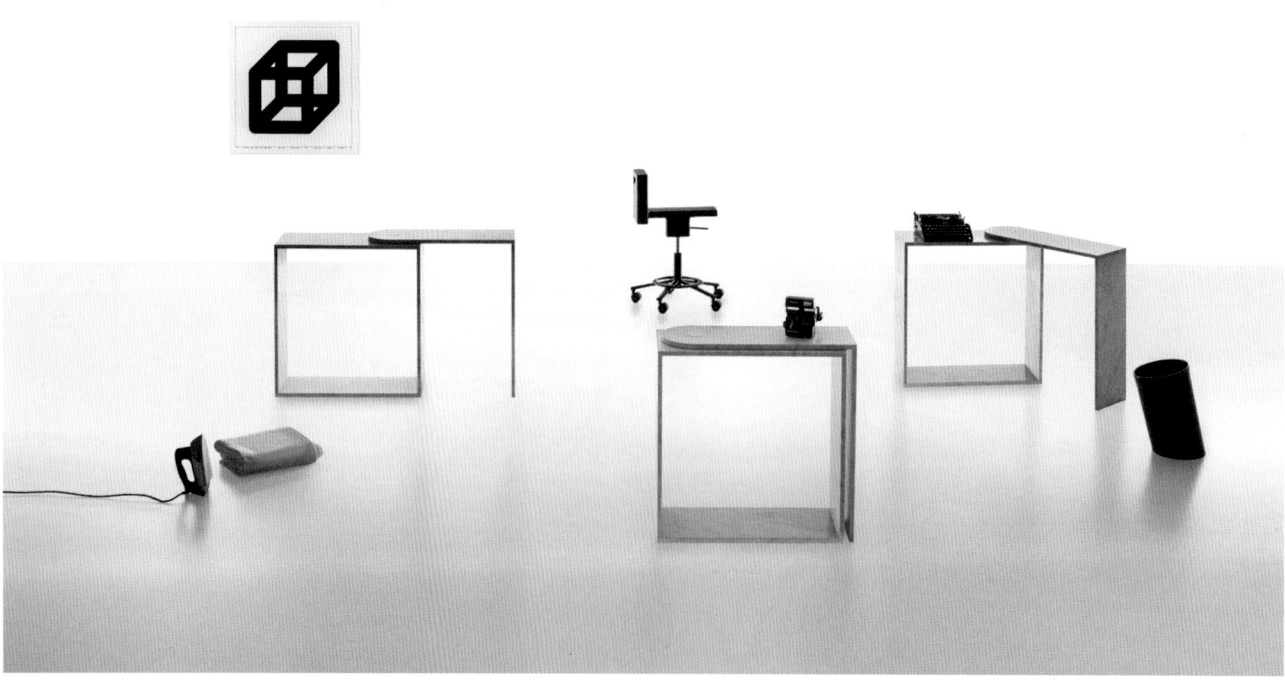

Among other brands, the designer has collaborated with the Italian manufacturer Marsotto Edizioni on specializing in a wide variety of designs in marble. Famous for its excellent quality combining ancient manual techniques with innovative production systems, the company has the history of more than two centuries. In creating their timeless pieces of furniture, homeware objects and lighting, they work with the world's most prominent designers and architects whose goal is to reinvent the use of marble by introducing an element of surprise.

Within the "Working on Marble" collection, commissioned by Marsotto Edizioni, Grcic designed a desk. As we associate marble with a rather solid material, the *Keyboard* table surprises us with its flexibility. The curved extension on the top rotates and thus allows for various configurations depending on our working place and needs. It was manufactured using white Carrara marble slabs. The piece is a minimal desk with a matt polished finish. Its clean lines provide practical space to work without dominating the space, even in its most extended position. Grcic challenges the marble's qualities and sets in motion what is actually heavy and solid. The choice of material is certainly an unorthodox one for a desk, but thanks to the simple yet practical silhouette, the visual effect is striking. It was invented by the designer and his project assistant, Charlotte Talbot, of the KGID. Marsotto Edizioni commissioned five other designers to create objects of Carrara marble, including Naoto Fukasawa and Jasper Morrison.

NEW TENDENCY
Hash Coat Rack, 2014

"With a profound belief in a design that creates cultural values, and in a design that satisfies intellectual, functional and poetic needs, New Tendency gives form to ideas for the now". This bold promise from the interdisciplinary Berlin-based design studio finds confirmation in their intriguing portfolio. While principles of Modernist design and Bauhaus traditions are at the core of their vision, they pride themselves on products that are handcrafted in Germany. Clean aesthetics and functional forms define the products by New Tendency. Under the creative direction of Manuel Goller, with Sebastian Schönheit as co-founder, the brand develops furniture and accessories in co-operation with carefully selected designers and architects. Goller and Schöncheit met when they were studying at the Bauhaus University in Weimar, Germany, and, from the beginning, the idea behind their inventive venture was to redefine the norms. The duo has been called "a contemporary face of

Bauhaus" by the professional press. "People often refer to the Bauhaus as rational and constructive, but I am really inspired by the poetic and spiritual tone of it as well." Goller explains.

Hash is a playful powder-coated steel coat rack. It consists of four steel rods that intersect and rest upon one another in the most surprising and eye-deceiving way. Two X-shaped elements actually look as if they were about to collapse but in reality, they are ready to take on the weight of coats, jackets and accessories. At the top of each rod, there is a notch for hangers, garments and bags. This simple combination of clean lines becomes an intriguing and capacious storage piece. In accordance with the brand's aims, the rack is both eye-catching and discrete. The original structure is functional and works well in various interiors thanks to its neutral form. Minimalist in style, it will work well in diverse environments. Accommodating today's nomadic style of life, *Hash* can be assembled and disassembled as the rods are produced individually, which makes interior arrangement much easier. The rack is available in a wide range of refined colours. As with other designs produced under the New Tendency label, this one is monochromatic and elegant. Restrained aesthetics are yet another hallmark of New Tendency influenced by the Bauhaus.

JULIEN DE SMEDT
Stoop, 2012 / Vestre

"Urban spaces should be humanly designed, politically engaged, financially viable, structurally realistic, and of course, skateable!" claimed Julien De Smedt, and to prove this thesis, designed *Stoop*, a public bench with multiple seating levels. The structure interacts dynamically with the surroundings and people can sit on its steps in a flexible and socializing way. The reference the designer's studio had in mind was a photo by Art Kane titled "A Great Day in Harlem" showing a gathering of famous jazzmen of the 20th century posing on a *stoop*. "Waiting in front of your friend's house on a *stoop* in Brooklyn, posing with a tourist group on the Spanish Steps in Rome, or having a picnic on the steps of the Sydney Opera House, we decided to incorporate the universal idea of using stairs as a sitting object, into our design of a bench." comments the designer. The stepped bench has a triangular shape and can serve as both a seat for a group of people or a table-bench.

De Smedt imagines the *Stoop* working well in various environments and finds the bench ideal for parents watching their children play games, for a professional meeting, or for lunch with colleagues. It can also be installed on schoolyards or university grounds for students to hang out with their friends, books or laptops. Yet another location would be in an urban space, the *Stoop* could act as a perfect meeting point on city squares. Its playful look and light, appealing structure are quite practical as it can add a touch of originality to any surrounding. De Smedt's urban auditorium is available in two types of surface, either wooden slats or recycled rubber, all designed for long-term use.

JDS / Julien De Smedt Architects is a multidisciplinary office focusing on architecture and design, from large scale planning to furniture. Founded by Julien De Smedt, it comprises a team of around 30 in offices in Copenhagen and Brussels. Their projects combine a fresh look at design issues with multiple expertise. "Regardless of scale, the studio outlines an approach that is affirmatively social in its outcome, enthusiastic in its ambition and professional in its process." they state.

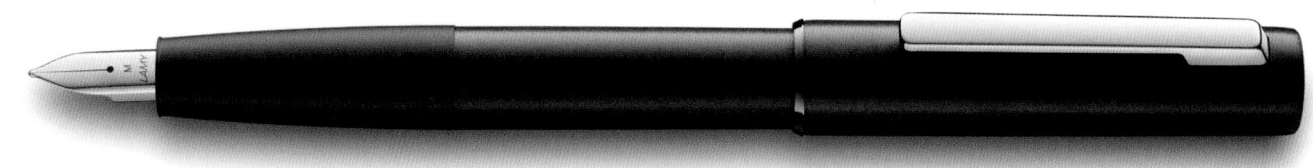

JASPER MORRISON
LAMY Aion, 2017 / LAMY

Aion is an aluminium pen with a silk-matt body, circular-brushed finish, blasted grip and newly designed expressive stainless-steel nib. It is available in a choice of two hues and three nibs (fountain pain, rollerball pen and ballpoint pen). The grip zone is matted, which is not only a visual accent, but also a practical solution to prevent the fingers from slipping. Created by British designer, Jasper Morrison, the pen initiates a new writing instrument series in the portfolio of LAMY. The manufacturer stresses the minimalist look: the sleek, perfectly-proportioned body, a straight clip and a stainless-steel spring. "At the same time, the LAMY *Aion* reveals an uncompromising modernity, which is especially visible in the details." explains the producer. "For the first time, a Lamy fountain pen has been equipped with a series-exclusive, newly-formed nib. Jasper Morrison gave it an unconventionally-proportioned outline, thus giving the writing instrument an avant-garde character." they add. The "cast in one piece" manufacturing process is an innovation developed by the brand in the production process. It makes the components seamless. Reducing the amount of plastic to the minimum, all *Aion* is manufactured by metal. Morrison's design celebrates the pleasure of writing by hand. As a lifestyle accessory, it is also an expression of the user's individual style.

Jasper Morrison is a graduate in design from Kingston Polytechnic and pursued postgraduate studies at the Royal College of Art. Since he established his London-based studio in 1986, the designer has collaborated with a number of manufacturers to develop furniture, kitchenware, electrical devices, accessories, lighting as well as storage solutions. Currently the studio has offices in London, Paris, and Tokyo. It realizes a number of projects across disciplines including the designs of brand's consultancies and exhibitions. The German brand LAMY is an iconic manufacturer who is famous for its high-quality writing tools, characterized by timeless aesthetics and perfect functionality. Founded in 1930, it has gained an international recognition for its clean and elegant designs that introduce a touch of class to writing. The trend-setting label produces over 8 million writing instruments a year. To keep surprising users with stylish new models, they regularly team up with famous designers.

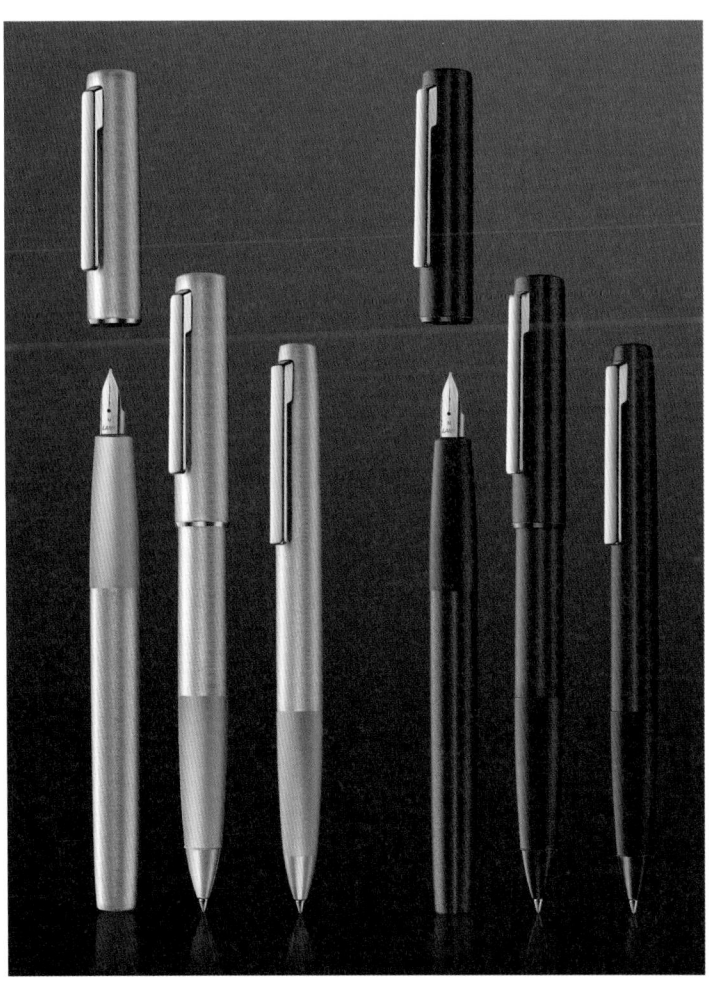

JEHS+LAUB
Hue, 2018 / Davis

Davis is a contract furniture company putting the stress on studying what interior designers and end users want and need. Their current range of projects focuses on comfort: "The feel and comfort of space, and how products work together to create comfort." The *Hue* collection of cases with its elegant lines and clean, architectural look by the German studio Jehs+Laub is emblematic of Davis' philosophy. The flexibility of the *Hue* concept — pursuing the sleek and the minimal, allows a lot of freedom in arranging an interior. Available with as low-boards, side-boards, high-boards and even wardrobes, each with a variety of options. The highly diverse series functions as a system adaptable to any interior, which depends on the user's needs. It does not only provide the storage, but also work as a simple and clean solution for separating spaces. The restrained design pleases the eye, but also merges smoothly with the environment. The classic form does not invade the space or force any particular style, and is thus unobtrusive. *Hue* becomes one with its surroundings, which is one of the designer's objectives. "Making something that works with everything very intuitively is not an easy task. The details are very subtle; we don't want it to mess with the environment." states the manufacturer in the same spirit. *Hue* is available with cases not only in two, three, four and five door widths but also in walnut, oak or in a choice of 26 new paint colours, a rainbow of hues to match any interior.

    Markus Jehn and Jürgen Laub met while studying industrial design at the Hochschule für Gestaltung Schwäbisch Gmünd. They established a common practice in 1994 after their graduation and an internship in New York. Furniture and lighting for the internationally renowned manufacturers dominate the duo's portfolio. They also design showrooms and interiors as well as exhibitions. Jehs+Laub experiments with forms and materials, which results in perfectly functional yet visually intriguing objects. That is particularly visible in the studio's inventive chair design. Comfort, a unique look, high-quality materials and design that looks effortless as well as natural within the space are the trademarks of the studio.

HARRI KOSKINEN
Genano 120, 2016 / Genano

Genano 120 is an air purifier, which impresses with its effective technology, and its minimalistic, elegant look. It results from the co-operation between two Finnish teams — designer Harri Koskinen and manufacturer Genano, established in 1999. The discovery of a new air purification method paved the way for this partnership. Meant for small spaces, its airflow can be adjusted with a 6-step manual control up to 120m^3 of fresh air per hour. Efficiency in reducing the health risks of airborne impurities is at the core of the design. "Our solutions can address even the most challenging air purification needs, ranging from battling against the spread of infectious diseases in healthcare facilities to securing safe study environment for children in schools with severely compromised indoor air quality." explains the producer. Thanks to an innovative, filter-free electric air decontamination technology, Genano 120 is able to purify the air from even nano-sized particles including viruses, bacteria, mould spores, or pollen-generated soot particles. The smart purifier is hidden in a classy and minimalistic casting of painted steel, which comes in four different colours. Its softly curved, slim yet tall silhouette balances the otherwise voluminous size of the device. *Genano 120*'s easy-to-use mode simply requires plugging into an electric outlet without any other installation. The user's only maintenance task is to change, approximately twice a year, the module collecting all airborne contaminants.

Koskinen is one of the leading names in the design community in Finland. A design director of the iconic Iittala brand since 2012, he has also worked for other Finnish and international manufacturers. Recognized for his bold aesthetics and conceptual approach, Koskinen seeks solutions that will be innovative for the consumer and producer as his goal. He starts work on new designs by exploring the essential aspects of the given commission, and then tries to "combine a strict and rational approach with more free and intuitive perspectives", as he calls it. Koskinen's designs are quintessentially Nordic in spirit. "In Scandinavia," he says, "we are generally brought up with enough mental space to explore our individuality while at the same time giving back to society." Exactly like the *Genano 120* air purifier, a device that can make a huge difference.

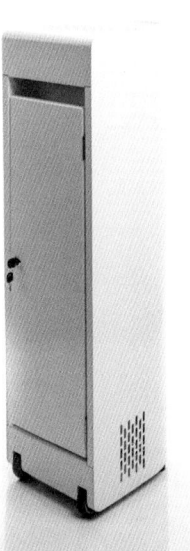

MARTIN ERICSSON
New Standard II, 2016

Martin Ericsson is a Gothenburg-based, and London-trained graphic designer who founded his design studio in 2000. Twelve years later, the practice has become a name in the furniture and product design sector for both domestic and public environments. Working with high-standard materials, environmental responsibility and co-operating with local manufacturers are at the heart of each project. Designs, while being durable and functional, should, in Ericsson's vision, also have a timeless expression. The focus is on simplicity and the uncluttered character of objects. This clean style obviously echoes Ericsson's background in graphic design. In 2015, the first self-produced furniture collection was developed and presented to the public. It was characterized by the interplay of straight lines and round shapes, and initiated an interesting process of developing the concepts by working with their proportions and silhouettes.

Ericsson's ladder *New Standard II*, designed one year later, is a light and elegant object that makes kitchen life more convenient. Designed to provide good stability when reaching kitchen shelves, it is also easy to move around. The structure is high enough to be functional, but low enough to be secure when climbing on it. The steps and the seat of the ladder are made of a solid ash and

steel construction. Visually, the idea was to contrast the bent shape of the tubular pipes with the back's bevelled edge. The angles of the legs are optimised for proper balance. The tactile feel is another important feature. While the wood has distinct graining, it is painted in soft matt tones just like the steel tubes. Users can select from five different hues to complement the furnishing in their kitchens. Practical for reaching the highest shelves, the ladder can also be used as an additional seat (between the 1950s and 1980s, a kitchen stool was a mainstay in many Swedish homes). Ironically, the shape of *New Standard's II* tubular base resembles the type of ladder used in swimming pools. Martin Ericsson invented it with kitchens in mind, but the timeless and elegant silhouette could be an unobtrusive element of any other room.

HENRIK PEDERSEN
Bar Cart, 2018 / Gloster Furniture

Henrik Pedersen was originally a graduate in fashion design. "Experience and knowledge help, but the difference lies in how you use it. Good common sense and a passion for your craft will take you far." he says boldly. Pedersen runs 365°, a Danish design studio based in Aarhus, which focuses on lifestyle-based designs, ranging from furniture to lighting. Exquisite materials and execution, formal clarity and attention to details are common in his realizations, but they are also fueled by extensive travel which allows the designer to keep up with market trends internationally. "For me, design must has a meaning. The shape, colour and choice of materials have to complement each individual design. Good design is functional, beautiful and easy to understand." states the designer.

Pedersen's *Bar Cart* for Gloster has a natural finish teak frame with stainless steel accents. This everyday object is both a practical and decorative element for a terrace or a garden. The cart can be helpful as an additional storage space, or as an oversized tray to serve drinks or snacks. The two tiers offer an extensive surface. The tiers' rhythmic texture and generous gaps between the slats make cleaning easier. The gently rounded edges on both trays (that also protect from spills) and the tubular structure they are placed on, soften the robust impression made by the wooden parts. The large-diameter wheels mean it moves smoothly, especially on uneven ground, which is another interesting element invented by Pedersen. A built-in handle ensures precise manoeuvring.

The *Bar Cart* exemplifies the manufacturer's philosophy: Gloster is a German brand dedicated to outdoor furniture combining great manufacturing and outstanding design. Their goal is the clients' pleasure, they claim. The teak used by the brand is produced on their own plantations. As a sign of their care for natural resources, they only harvest what they have planted themselves (each Gloster teak tree has a lifecycle of at least 50 years!). The designs are conceived in collaboration with world-renowned designers. "Once a concept is approved, designers work closely with the development team at our factory to further refine their designs." the manufacturer declares.

#6

GOOD DESIGN IS HONEST

"It does not make a product more innovative, powerful or valuable than it really is. It does not attempt to manipulate the consumer with promises that cannot be kept."

Dieter Rams

Throughout his career, Dieter Rams has refused any kind of artificiality. Neither in the way design is perceived as a discipline ("design is not simply an adjective to place in front of a product's name to somehow artificially enhance its value." he emphasizes), nor in any kind of manipulation that could deceive the customer. While there are many ways to make a product look much more impressive than it is in reality, an honest approach is actually the starting point for all other principles of good design mentioned here. Each stage of the design process should be focused on precision and quality, but also managed by a straightforward way of thinking. Only then will innovation come along to make a product powerful and valuable quite naturally. Honesty in design also determines the relationship between the designers, manufacturers and users.

JAIME HAYON
Wings Bed, 2017 / Wittmann

Jaime Hayon's *Wings Bed* for the Austrian manufacturer Wittmann is the essence of bed design. The Spanish designer, famous for his whimsical imagery, employs all his signature features — shapes invented with creativity and curiosity, great sense of proportions and a perfect eye for combined materials in this bed. Sweet dreams come easily on wings... humorously states the design's description. Two characteristic tiltable additions on either side of the bed's head create the effect of an embrace. The bed is conceived here as a place for spending time, not just for sleeping. Equipped with leather-covered, built-in bedside tables as well as moveable LED spotlights for reading, it is a comfortable platform. Its sensual curves and generous upholstery make it a warm and cosy cocoon, be it to sleep at night or spend time in during the day. "It is important to remember that my design is made for humans — to be used by humans. I believe that design should provoke emotions. Design should make you feel good. Create happiness." says enthusiastically Hayon. *Wings Bed* certainly does.

Hayon studied industrial design in Madrid and Paris. In 1997 he joined Fabrica, a design and communication academy founded by Benetton, and worked closely with the legendary Oliviero Toscani. The talented Hayon soon became the head of their Design Department. Hayon established his own practice in 2000 but it was only after 2003 he fully dedicated himself to personal projects. Initially featuring toys, ceramics and furniture, the portfolio was expanded to include interior design and installations. The studio currently operates

with offices in Italy, Spain and Japan. "Hayon cherishes admiration for a design era with which Wittmann is also closely linked: the time of the Wiener Werkstätte, the era of Josef Hoffmann who brought a new freshness into the buildings of the Viennese bourgeoisie with his holistic approach to the early 20th century." stresses the manufacturer, whose ambition is also to make furniture that can be passed to the next generation. Wittmann itself is a family-owned company in the fourth generation. In terms of design, the focus is on elegance, balance and durability with awareness of quality and artisanship. Founded in 1896 as a saddlery, the brand has developed an impressive collection of furniture created in collaboration with some of the finest designers.

CHARLOTTE JUILLARD
Baskets Sacot, 2017 / Ligne Roset

French designer Charlotte Juillard is one of the young talents on the design scene. After studying design and interior architecture at the École Camondo, she undertook an industrial design exchange with the University of Montreal. The designer's degree project was realized in partnership with the prestigious Manufacture de Sèvres. In 2012, she joined the Benetton's Fabrica and worked on a number of projects for the brand. 2014 marked her return to Paris and the starting point of her own creative studio to design across disciplines, including scenography projects. "She believes in the importance of handwork in which the craftsman's knowledge becomes the center of a project. Her pieces are part of a sustainability's research where textures and forms, softness and femininity combine in favor of the same ambition, giving evidence to the object." points out her statement. Juillard's distinctive style is based on a sophisticated play of forms, clear lines and surprising, yet very attractive combinations of materials. Whether a ceramic loud speaker, a mirror wearing textured fringes or lighting with only the skeletons of lampshades, extravagant ideas are not uncommon in the designer's portfolio.

In collaboration with Ligne Roset, Juillard designed a small storage basket *Sacot*, which signifies a leather bag in Provençal. The designer made it to perfectly store magazines or toys, but also to use in a hallway, a living room, beneath a desk or on a bedside table. The minimal form and elegant hue will match any kind of interior. The basket is also ideally shaped and sized (17 x 40 x 40 cm) to easily move small items from one space to another. "This project was arose from a desire to make an object with a minimum of intervention during its creation." comments the designer. Consequently, *Sacot* was created without the need of sewing. To keep the shape firm, there is a coloured cord that is both an elegant visual accent as well as the only element to assemble. The leather is black and the cord comes in gray.

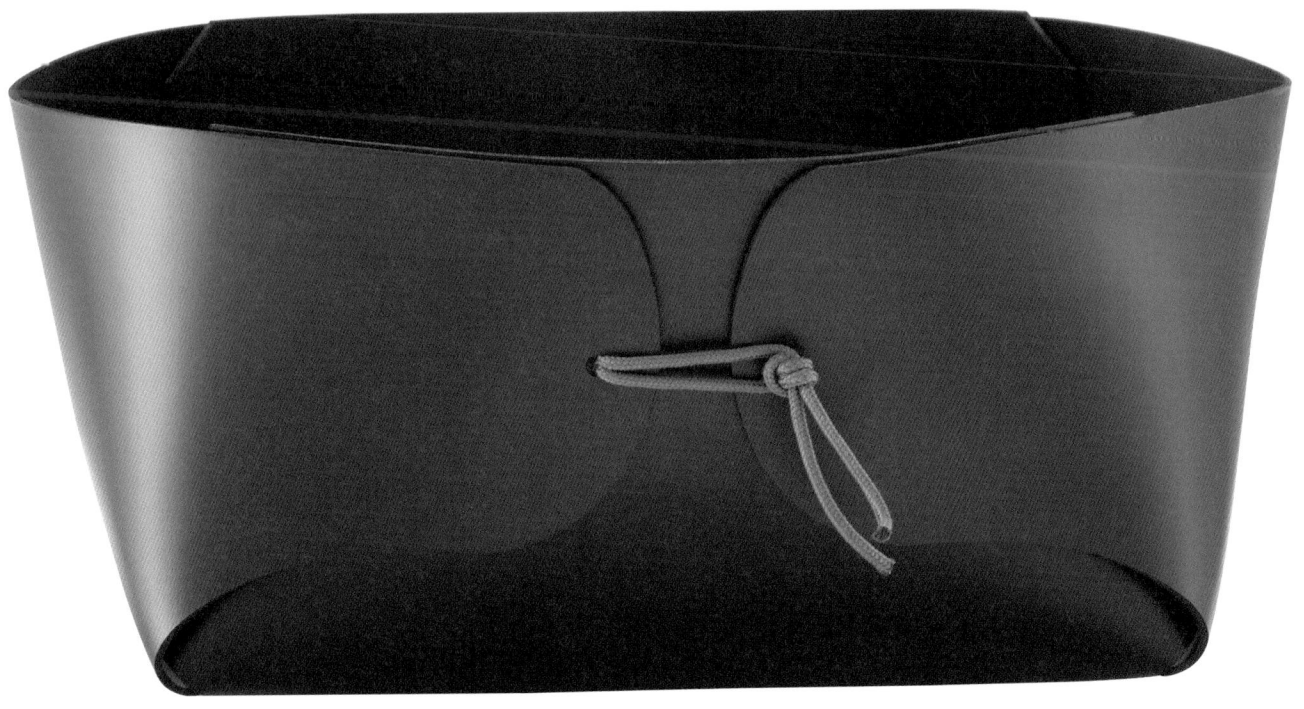

HELLA JONGERIUS
Seat Dots, 2016 / Vitra

The vivid *Seat Dots* are simple, eye-catching and functional designs by Hella Jongerius for Vitra. With their comfortable upholstery padding, they are designed to fit a wide range of chairs. Jongerius, a Dutch designer, is famous for her ongoing research on colours, materials and textures, which is clearly evident in this particular project. These round cushions, available in a wide selection of both vivid and subdued hues, provide an enhanced seating comfort. They can add a subtle chromatic touch or, on the contrary, be bold elements of any interior decor. In any case, these dots are always trendy and fun. The rounded shape intensifies the colour's effect and makes it more visible in the surroundings. Hence the *Seat Dots* are simple and minimal in form but nevertheless expressive. "Colour touches so many different aspects of design: words, shapes, materials, physics, space, light. The experience of colour is completely dependent on its physical, visual, artistic and cultural context." says the designer. One practical feature of the *Seat Dots* is that each cushion can be used on both sides and washed.

Berlin-based Jongeriuslab was established in 1993 to generate projects in various fields, from fabrics, ceramics and furniture to interior design. The significance of colour is at the heart of the multifaceted practice, perhaps because the designer's mother worked as a pattern maker, and so from an early age she was surrounded by piles of fabric. Jongerius has been the Art Director for colours and materials at Vitra for many years, resulting in the development of the Vitra Colour & Material Library. It is used as "a system that enables the versatile combination of different materials and colours throughout the extensive Vitra product collection", explains the manufacturer. Jongerius conducted an intensive study of the qualities and possibilities of colour and texture in textiles as well as in other materials. The designer also analysed hundreds of products and compared the hues of existing Vitra products with the original specifications in the archives to see the way the brand's design evolved over the years. This interesting task inspired the designer to write a book describing the complex process, which she titled "I Don't Have a Favourite Colour".

AYTM
Unity Tray, 2017

Kathrine and Per Gran Hartvigsen, the couple who has run the company Gran Living ApS since 2004, created a new brand, AYTM, to reinvent Danish luxury design by experimenting with innovative materials and a new colour palette. They focus on high-quality homeware products that would be surprising in their novelty and please the eye with fresh aesthetics but also stand the test of time. AYTM's collections are designed by a talented, in-house team of designers, craftsmen and engineers, who were invited to join forces and bring their experience, to help diversify the range of products. The effect is very Nordic in style, in form and in the use of original hues, which are both balanced and simple. However, AYTM's approach to Nordic design is much more expressive. "We wanted every single piece to be unique and eye-catching, but it has also been important that all the products together look like a collection and create a spectacular atmosphere." the brand comments.

The *Unity Tray*, cut from solid brass, is a very elegant option for decorating the home. "Strong visual effects are created when the mix of materials, colours and shapes come together in perfect harmony." says the studio. Employing geometry in a playful way, the series consists of three elements: quarter circles in different sizes and one half-circle-piece. Each component of the collection can be used as a regular tray, but they can also work as decorative display elements. Put together in various configurations (*Unity Tray* comes in different shapes, colours and sizes to provide flexibility), they create a chromatically contrasting composition that will look unique on every table. The design is available in several deep hues, like gold, silver, dusty green or bordeaux. Powder-coated iron with a shiny or matt finish adds a touch of elegance. Making the best use of AYTM's signature graphic lines, the tray's functional and aesthetic aspects are perfectly fused.

The brand's collections for home interiors are primarily designed for the dining room, living room and kitchen, but the *Unity Tray* can be used anywhere.

THOMAS BERNSTRAND
+ LINDAU & BORSELIUS
Honken Bench, 2015 / Blå Station

 The *Honken* series was designed for the Swedish furniture manufacturer Blå Station in the context of the Experiment 2015 project, which was an open design process involving designers Thomas Bernstrand (the main designer), Stefan Borselius and Johan Lindau. Based on one brief, it resulted in three different products. The highlight of the collection is the spacious *Honken* armchair, which can also be used as an intimate sofa for two. Its elegant, transparent sheet metal structure sits on turned legs of solid oak, which are common elements in the series. The *Honken* bench can be used in numerous ways — together with the table from the collection, as a coffee table or simply as an individual seat. Unlike the armchair, the whole body is made of solid wood. The lacquered steel fasteners at the top of the legs are the only visual accent. The simplicity and compactness of the bench are striking. The combination of high-quality craftsmanship with the timeless beauty of solid wood results in sculptural forms that are strong, aesthetic, and long lasting. The playful angles of the legs, the designer's only extravagant touch, add some lightness to the structure. The *Honken* range also consists of a table and a round coffee table.

Thomas Bernstrand, the main designer of the collection, graduated from a long list of schools, where he studied crafts, design and industrial design. While his approach is deeply functional, the designer creates objects that users can genuinely interact with in everyday life. Stefan Borselius studied furniture carpentry (following his skilled grandfather and great grandfather) and design. "When he works with a product, Stefan Borselius leaves nothing to chance, but goes methodically and wholeheartedly through every single detail, every function and every characteristic which a material or a technique can offer." comments the manufacturer Blå Station. Johan Lindau is the manufacturer's design manager and CEO with great knowledge of materials, techniques and industrial processes. His goal is to offer simple, effective and functional solutions. Therefore, the designers Lindau chooses to work with, should not only have conviction, dedication and insight, but also take design seriously. The three designers often team up to share their diverse talents and extensive experience in designing furniture.

STEFAN DIEZ
New Order 2.0, 2014 / Hay

With the designer's focus on versatility, the *New Order* collection, made of interconnecting aluminium parts, is a very flexible system for working spaces. As all its elements are modular, it offers endless combinations of shelving and storage arrangements. *New Order 2.0*, an even more flexible, updated version, was developed by DIEZ OFFICE in collaboration with the HAY team. The collection grew bigger with the addition of tables, panels, drawers and doors, as well as workspace management solutions. Initially meant for home offices, the extended system was created with busy and ever-changing office environments in mind. The designer's goal is to provide tools that allow more effective engagement with one's workspace. The system is unbiased, thanks to the elements like panels or doors and it can be mounted and be accessed from all sides. This adaptable system, designed by Stefan Diez, brought many ingenious solutions for the WeWork network of shared offices. *New Order* functions as a space-divider and space-creator while helping to organize the space in-between in a functional, elegant and rational way.

Visually light, all components are also extremely durable and precisely executed. The collection's graphic lines contribute to its minimalistic look. "*New Order* is born of 100% industrial production, reflecting our ambition to create uncompromising quality products." asserts the manufacturer. Airy, open structures can be combined with closed and compact constructions; panels, trays, shelves, drawers, sliding doors or screens give lots of scope for creative and open-ended configurations, which, on the top of this, can be easily adjusted whenever a new arrangement is needed.

München-based designer Stefan Diez founded his own studio in 2002, which he concisely describes: "The practice of Diez Office is characterized by innovation through technical expertise, instinct and a passion for experimentation." The designer was born into a family of four generations of carpenters, which influenced his future career: He started studies in industrial design after being trained as a cabinetmaker. Supported by his team, as well as local craftsmen and specialists, Diez explores a broad spectrum of projects effectively transforming bold concepts into products. Regardless of the discipline. Diez's aesthetic approach is clean, precise and minimalistic.

MATALI CRASSET
Twist La Vie, 2017 / Tex, Carrefour

TEX, which is the textile label of the French supermarket chain Carrefour, was commissioned Matali Crasset to create a collection embracing the seasons of the year. The French designer received carte blanche from the brand: the only constraint was that each part of the series was to be unveiled separately. "Twist life" became the leitmotiv for all of them to inspire optimism. "The collection proposes a joyful approach to life, inviting all to share, meet and express themselves through the generous tints of flat colours." says Crasset. The highlight of the first offerin was the theme of "Around the Home". Alluding to the spring when it had its premiere, the ornamental motifs were inspired by the organic world. The designer created a linear pattern informed by the branches of a plant growing with energy and expanding into a complex graphic composition. "I decided to develop a pattern inspired by a vegetal pattern, because the vegetal is a common, shared language. It anchors itself deeply as a design inspiration." explains the designer. "The vegetal is a metaphor for life." she adds. Among around 20 different items for various rooms in the home, there is a set of three towels, the texture of which adds an even more intriguing effect to the rhythmical pattern, especially as the towels are monochromatic. The designer, however, plays with the hues and, adds contrasting edges, so that the towels in all three colours work as a harmonic set. Last but not least, the attractively priced collection (an aspect particularly important for the designer) was created using high-quality, sustainable textiles.

    Crasset is graduated from Les Ateliers – École Nationale Supérieure de Création Industrielle in Paris, where she studied marketing and industrial design. After working with Denis Santachiara in Milan, and Philippe Starck back in Paris, the designer opened her own studio in 1998, which was followed by establishing the company Matali Crasset Production four years later. She states that her work is "a refusal of the pure shape", and Crasset explores very diverse disciplines, from scenography to furniture, from handicraft to electronics, from graphics to interior design. Modularity and flexibility are some of the leading themes in her designs.

ROGER VANCELLS
Milano, 2016 / Made Design

The oversized, wall-mounted coat hooks designed by Roger Vancells for Made Design, Barcelona, is a part of the *Milano* collection. In addition to a coat stand with a light structure of six curved beech-wood slats arranged in a radial fashion, the designer also re-invented the hook. Made of wood, the hook exemplifies minimalism with a twist. This strongly elongated and thin rectangular hook sinks into the surface of the wall. Its rounded edges provide a smooth visual effect. Only the top is slightly bent for hanging clothing. The hook's proportions are the most interesting element here: while hooks are normally small objects, in Vancells' version they have substantial dimensions: 34 x 4 x 10 cm. The hooks offer a simple solution in a sculptural shape. Their light structure is, at the same time, a practical support in everyday life. Playing with the size, the designer not only achieves an unusual look that challenges our perception, but also make the design more stability. Stronger hooks can carry much heavier things without the danger of collapsing and damaging the wall.

Barcelona-based Vancells devoted his practice to designing products and environments. Educated as an industrial designer at ESDAP LLotja and Escola Massana, he always aims at approaching design in a new and coherent way. "The method of work is transversal, based on experience, and is focused on using design as a tool to reveal the beauty of everyday life, with attractive, functional, unique solutions and the result of a constant search to reach innovation." comments the designer. Vancells' portfolio consists of furniture, lighting, packaging, electronics as well as retail, corporate and exhibition spaces plus ephemeral installations. Together with Miquel Angel Julià, the designer runs a cross-disciplinary design studio, Nuklee, based in Barcelona. Made Design Barcelona, established in 2010, produces accessories for home, office and public spaces in collaboration with renowned designers.

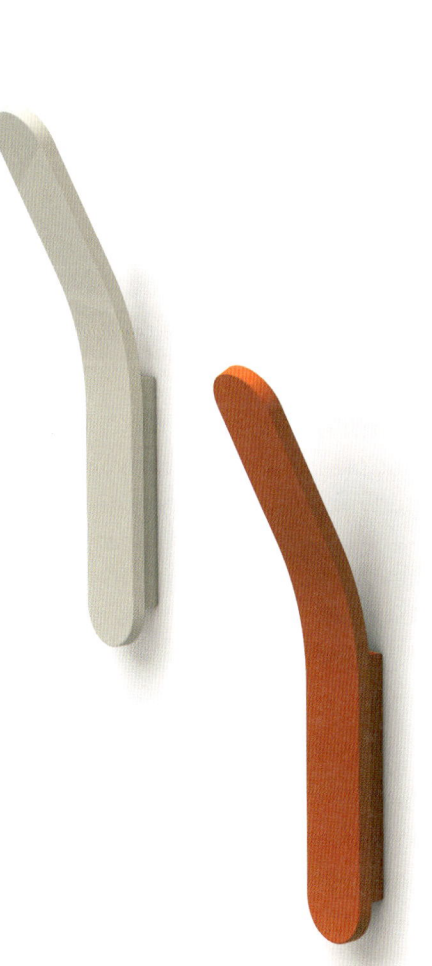

MARC VENOT AND ANTOINE LESUR
Festival, 2013

"Tomorrow, we will be old!" warns Marc Venot (born in 1979!), and, together with Antoine Lesur, the French designer exploring a design that could ease aging. "We took an interest in this object that becomes an essential companion when getting older: the walking stick." he says. Design, comfort and ergonomics are at the core of this collection of four prototypes. The idea was to create a structure that, in a similar way to a piece of furniture, could bear the body and, like a prosthesis, would be its extension. To both designers it was extremely important that the walking sticks shouldn't be limited only to their practical role, but could also be a source of aesthetic pleasure. Issues with walking in old age can be disturbing, and accepting one's decline is difficult. Venot and Lesur believed that this process would be less stressful if the sticks were aesthetically designed. The fresh, original look of the sticks could encourage people to use them and accept them as a stylish accessory rather than a display of disability. Venot and Lesur have, herewith, taken walking sticks to a new level. The creation of the four prototypes (elle, elonie, harry and jerry) was preceded by extensive testing sessions in pursuit of the most ergonomic form. Each model is an elegant and engaging walking support. Slim yet solid, executed of materials such as wood, leather or aluminium, with various top elements, the sticks are shaped well. Bends, proportions and grips adjust to the physiology of the human body, and individual comfort.

Paris-based Marc Venot firstly graduated in maths and physics to continue his education in industrial design. After graduating from École Nationale Supérieure de Création Industrielle, he worked for a French Global design agency specializing in luxury brands. 2011 marked the opening of his own studio, where the projects range from furniture to product design. Venot's works combine sophistication and a great sense of imagination. The designer plays with forms and materials to reinvent well-known objects and offer a fresh perspective. After graduating from École Boulle, Antoine Lesur worked for 10 years in various agencies, half of that time at Patrick Jouin's studio. In 2012 he established his individual practice to explore various disciplines from product and furniture to space design.

MARK DAY
Debit Card, 2018 / Starling Bank

Starling's Art Director, Mark Day, rotated a debit card by 90 degrees and applied a modern and simple layout to this new format. The vertical design is advertised as a sign of the times by this digital-only bank, which operates primarily through a mobile app. "Design usually evolves to solve something or to meet new needs, and bank cards don't look the way they do by accident." remarks Day. "They were designed in the landscape format because of the way old card machines worked, and they're embossed with raised numbers so they could be printed onto a sales voucher. But we don't use those machines anymore, so when you think about it, a landscape-format card is just a solution to a 'problem' that no longer exists." he adds. The idea behind the project is practical and aims at re-shaping card design for the way we actually use them. Today, whether we pay at the checkout counter or withdraw cash from an ATM, we tend to operate our cards in a vertical, portrait position. Interestingly, the rear of Day's card is still in the landscape format to make the transition easier, perhaps, or maybe just because the back includes all the relevant information and a landscape format is easier to read.

Starling Bank is the first UK bank to launch a vertically designed debit card. However, there are banks, which have already introduced this format, like Virgin America, Credit Union and Capital One. Many see the customer-friendly portrait card as just a gimmick, but it does make slotting a card into an ATM or a card machine much more instinctive. "Good design is about more than the way things look. It's about challenging old methods and responding to cultural shifts," comments Day, "adapting the outdated to meet new ways of living."

#7

GOOD DESIGN IS LONG-LASTING

"It avoids being just fashionable and therefore never appears outdated. Unlike the fashionable design, it lasts for many years — even in today's throwaway society."

Dieter Rams

The rapidly changing lifestyle and galloping technical progress inherent to it are not really conducive to a long-lasting approach, but rather encourage consumerism. Trends have become seasonal and encourage us to change styles on a regular basis. In addition, technology tends to change so quickly that we are often forced to purchase a newer model. "I imagine our current situation will cause future generations to shudder at the thoughtlessness in the way in which we today fill our homes, our cities, and our landscape with a chaos of assorted junk." warned Rams. We do indeed live in an age of waste. Rethinking the way we live and treat the environment has never been as crucial as it is today. Designing for the future should by all means be sustainable so as to preserve natural resources. But it should also serve for a long period of time, particularly in the case of appliances for personal use, to reduce the growing piles of debris.

FRANÇOIS AZAMBOURG
Grillage, 2012 / Ligne Roset

Easily folded, like a piece of origami, *Grillage* (which in French means wire mesh) is made of a perforated metal sheet. The sheet was stretched to create a mesh that was then folded and placed on a bent steel frame. Thanks to the ergonomic shape of both the sofa and the armchair that comprises the collection, and despite the rather sturdy material, the design is comfortable to use. François Azambourg challenges metal to create a light and subtle silhouette that will integrate with the surroundings. Outdoors, the perforated structure plays with the rays of the sun. *Grillage* can be also covered with a special, quilted cover matching the shape perfectly. Magnets sewn into the fabric make it easy to use. Although it is suitable for both indoor and outdoor use, this all-metal furniture is mostly seen on terraces and in gardens, which puts the material again into focus, this time due to its durability and functionality.

Resistant to any weather conditions the material will last for many years. Through all the production stages — stretching, folding and creasing, the collection celebrates the manufacturing process and stresses its complexity. "To manufacture *Grillage*, a sheet of metal, which is grooved in staggered rows, is stretched." the manufacturer explains, "Metal wire is then soldered to the exterior, piece by piece. The sheet thus obtained is folded at various points to create the seat: this is a manual operation which renders each armchair 'unique'. The shape of the armchair will evolve over time."

The designer's educational path was very interesting and diverse: Electrotechnical training at high school was followed by fine art studies at the École Nationale Supérieure des Beaux-Arts and later applied art at ENSAAMA — Olivier de Serres in Paris. This inspiring fusion of art and technique is visible in his ingenious designs influenced by his extensive knowledge of materials and manufacturing. Azambourg pushes the boundaries of both.

NORM ARCHITECTS
Steel Wall Clock, 2017 / Menu

Copenhagen-based Norm Architects was established by Jonas Bjerre-Poulsen and Kasper Rønn Von Lotzbeck in 2008. Together with their talented team, they work in the fields of industrial design and residential architecture, and also commercial interiors, photography and art direction. The studio draws from the traditions of Scandinavian design and cherishes timeless aesthetics, natural materials, as well as Modernist principles of restraint and refinement. In their designs, they focus on quality, details and durability "Through exploring what it is that heightens the human senses regardless of personal preference, our projects strip spaces, objects, ideas and images back to their simplest form. Our expertise lies in finding the balance — when there's nothing more to either add or take away." they say.

Quite consequently, *Steel Wall Clock* embodies their philosophy that simplicity carries bigger ideas. Reduced to the minimum, its round face is adorned only with basic hands. Focusing only on the essential elements produces a stunning effect. The clock is visible and discreet at the same time. Its pure, yet strong form draws our attention as we need a moment's concentration to read the time as the face lacks numbers. Menu, a Copenhagen-based manufacturer whose mission is to make the world better and less complicated with their designs, praises the clock for giving a new meaning to the word "timeless". There is, however, one more layer of timelessness, which is not based on stripping the form of hours and minutes: The high quality of materials makes the clock an ever-lasting object, thus transforming it into a timeless design. The clock is available in mirror-polished steel, brushed-brass and marble versions. "With smartphones replacing traditional watches in our society, we'd like to see a renaissance of the classic wall clock, an object not only beautiful but also highly distinguished." explains Bjerre-Poulsen. If anything could cause the comeback of the clock, it is surely the restrained, and dramatic design by Norm Architects. The designer's clock with its elegant and classic appearance can display the time in any interior, be it at home, a workspace or in public.

NORMAL STUDIO
Panbeton® Delicate, 2017 /
Concrete LCDA

The delicate art of origami influenced *Delicate*, which defines a new era in wall decoration. A concrete decorative panel, developed by Normal Studio for Concrete LCDA within the *Panbeton®* collection, *Delicate* is a wall cladding with a front face made of raw concrete and an ultra-light foam in the back. This structure allows for easy transportation and quick installation, while the concrete makes the wall cladding durable. *Panbeton®* is an innovative technology of ultra-light concrete invented to support the reviving fascination with brutalism and its minimalistic, timeless qualities. "We created a panel by making fine imprints in the concrete. After many experiments, we settled on a folding technique in order to render the delicateness of a sheet of paper when folded, and we developed a process that reveals the full subtlety of the folds and layers." state the designers, "The geometric pattern formed by the folds covers the entire surface of the panel, causing the viewer's eye to lose itself in the clever composition of this concrete sheet. Over a large area, the pattern generates a vibration that plays with the lighting. When light skims over the panel, the patterns appear, when in direct light, they fade away." Each single panel is 2600 x 90 mm in size, weighs 35 kilos and is available in 7 different colours and 3 finishes.

Jean-François Dingjian and Eloi Chafaï stand behind the Normal Studio. They founded their practice in 2006. Their main goal is to promote elementary design characterized by precise shapes. While working across disciplines, in different scales and with various materials, the duo is primarily interested in "transferring technologies between different worlds", as they call it. Formal research of an object is not at the heart of their designs, but rather the tool that generates the shape. As they strongly believe in the social and culture values of design, they opt for timeless pieces that will resist temporary trends. The Concrete LCDA (originally set up as LCDA in 2003) was relaunched in 2011, when three young entrepreneurs, Julien Gay, Julien & Valentin Delalande, took over the operations, and renowned designer Matali Crasset became the brand's artistic director, a position she held until 2015. They produce fibre-reinforced concrete interior fittings, and have also launched contemporary furniture.

BOWER STUDIOS
Duo Server , 2017

Bower is a New York-based multidisciplinary studio co-founded by Danny Giannella, Tammer Hijazi, and Jeffrey Renz, who named their studio after a bird known for creating beautiful and colourful structures. The team specializes in furniture and product design with a focus on mirrors. "Of all the things we surround ourselves with every day, the mirror is most closely related to our consciousness — a humble technology for understanding ourselves." they say. Their works, particularly mirrors, offer unexpected visual effects as a result of exploring our perceptions of depth and light. Bower's experiments lead to innovative and sophisticated interpretations of everyday objects. Their products often challenge the way we see things. Rather than pursuing the obvious, the studio's work is driven by curiosity and a spirit of discovery.

Bower designs accessories that are inspired by the shapes of their furniture line. The functional, and decorative objects for home or office are often executed in a similar range of materials. The *Duo Server* is a fine combination of noble marble and natural wood, making the best of both materials' natural properties, to prepare or serve food. While the wood piece is meant for cutting or displaying bread or meat, the marble circle is ideal for serving cheese. The design is thus convenient to use, and aesthetically pleasing. Placed on a table, this portable kitchen workshop turns into a stylish decorative object. The juxtaposition of contrasting materials is not the only reason for this eye-pleasing effect: it is the way that Bower's design plays with forms that also contributes to the aesthetic value of the board. Its simple shape with the twist of a marble circle nesting into a wooden board creates an intriguing, and elegant cylindrical form. Each of the two elements can also be used separately, adding to its practical aspect. However, they look best when they enhance each other. Solid wood and marble are some of the most long-lasting materials. Their natural qualities make each piece of the *Duo Server* unique.

DAVID ADJAYE
MA770 Wireless Speaker, 2017 / Master & Dynamic

The goal of Master & Dynamic, a brand launched by Jonathan Levine in 2014, is to provide creative minds with beautifully crafted and technically sophisticated sound tools. Going exclusively for the highest-quality materials, Master & Dynamic wants to create durable pieces that can be used for decades. The perfect balance of aesthetics, ease of use, and rich sound are also at the core of the designs and add to the iconic character of the brand's products. Every object in the brand's portfolio shares a common DNA, according to the manufacturer, which is characterised by a focus on great design, luxury materials, amazing craftsmanship and uncompromising performance. "We believe mastery is a never-ending exploration requiring a dynamic approach. Sound is a catalyst and a powerful creative element, helping to focus, inspire, and transport your mind." they explain.

All of these qualities are visible in the *MA770 Wireless Speaker* realized in collaboration with British architect, David Adjaye, who utilized a concrete composite material developed by Master & Dynamic. In addition to enhancing the object's durability, concrete — an unusual material for electronic devices — also contributes to optimising the acoustic potential. The concrete's properties prevent vibrations, thus improving the quality of sound. Adjaye's main idea was to redefine the home speaker, which he envisioned in a shape going far beyond traditional box speakers. "I became fascinated with the idea of using triangles to break down the mass of the box, and to see if we could dissolve the sense of volume through sculptural detail." the architect said. The sculptural silhouette is truly sensational: It's like having a small piece of architecture at home, which accidentally also transmits sound. The *MA770* can function as an individual stereo unit, or be paired with another speaker equipped with innovative technology for stereo, which is operated by digital media-streaming software Chromecast.

David Adjaye has run Adjaye Associates since 2000. The global, multicultural team of talented professionals has realized some of most impressive architectural projects around the world, with a strong belief that architecture presents opportunities for transformation. Working in different scales, Adjaye Associates use designing products and furniture as a testing ground for forms and materials.

SMARIN
sChaise, 2017

Smarin is a French design studio founded by designer Stéphanie Marin in 2003. It specializes in high-end furniture, with all pieces being manufactured at the studio's own workshop, based in Nice. "The heart of the concept behind the studio is to research and offer products made of natural and durable materials." reads their mission. Design, according to the studio, should be accessible and sustainable. While developing new projects, be they textiles, set design or space planning, Smarin teams up with designers, artists and personalities to diversify their approach and to enrich the brainstorming. Their works, often playful, fuse art and design in an interesting way, like the *sChaise* deck chair, which offers an alternative to usually hard outdoor furniture. As stressed by the designer, it is the chair that follows the body and not the other way around. At the same time, thanks to its flexibility and ergonomic shape, it is meant to improve bad sitting habits.

A tubular frame in pastel colours is wrapped with elastic straps, soft enough to accommodate the body. The deck chair is light and solid at once. "The *sChaise* is a research on the flexibility of the seat, the right posture and its effects." comments the designer. As such, it is supposed to stimulate the blood circulation and allow the body to cool down thanks to its airy structure. "I focused on the feeling of the body," added Marin, "and made a seat which allows the body to be unrestrained and find a natural position for the back, the muscles and for blood circulation." she explains, as the body's functions and well-being are her priorities. This is also the reason why the form of the piece is so scaled back and adaptable. Stéphanie Marin was invited by the Centre Georges Pompidou to unveil the *sChaise* in the context of a touring retrospective exhibition devoted to the work of David Hockney, which was shown at the museum. On this occasion, Smarin invited the visitors to participate in Bounce Station, a collective performance with the *sChaise*.

E15
DOTTO, 2015

Studio e15, cofounded by architect Philipp Mainzer and under the art direction of designer Farah Ebrahimi, was established in 1995. Named after the postal code of the brand's first workshop, located at the time in London, it is currently based in Frankfurt am Main and considered one of the best German design practices. e15 gained international recognition for the pioneering use of solid wood in pure form for their initial collections. The radical style was an expression of a new simplicity. Consistent and progressive design, highest-quality materials, as well as innovative, handcrafted production methods are all at the core of the e15 realizations. Whether designing furniture, lighting or accessories, the brand celebrates essential forms, which is expressed in a novel way. The company's sense of proportions and great feeling for materials lead to experimental and fresh designs. e15 develops original products in close cooperation with designers, architects and artists.

A strong environmental awareness is in the brand's DNA. "At e15, all products are developed with the goal to create long-lasting, quality and timeless designs." they emphasize. *DOTTO* is a statement blanket that is suitable for all seasons. Manufactured in Belgium, it is made of wool (71%) and cotton (29%). Its dimensions are 190 x 130 centimetres and it has a unique surface feel. "Spun atop a white cotton base, the dots are made of red, blue or black wool yarn creating a strong pattern." describes the manufacturer. The characteristic dotted texture, identical on both sides of the blanket, creates an attractive visual effect. Additionally, the edges are finished with a chunky white stitch, which is a practical way to prevent fraying. Each end of the blanket features dense yet short fringing as a reference to the traditional craft. Be it used as a cosy cover on the sofa or an additional layer on the bed, or outdoors on a chilly evening, this tactile throw will both look appealing and provide comfort. Its complex yet rhythmical pattern is available in three colour versions: blue, red or black. *DOTTO* seems like a good idea regardless of the time of year.

TOM DIXON
Brew Milk Pan, 2017

The *Brew Milk Pan* is part of the *Brew* family, which celebrates "coffee making as a form of art and coffee drinking as one of our few remaining contemporary rituals", as summed up by the designer-cum-manufacturer, Tom Dixon. With each step of the coffee making process in mind, the *Brew* series includes tools of exceptional quality for making perfect coffee. The collection is made of stainless steel with a film of vaporised copper. The copper creates an elegant high-shine gleam with reflective effects. Seamlessly executed, all elements of the *Brew* collection are visually striking and add a touch of class to any kitchen, café or table, not to mention the pleasure of brewing coffee with the help of such refined and beautiful tools. The sophisticated yet practical design of the *Brew* objects turns the routine of making coffee into a unique experience. In a way, it is a nod to the past when ceremonies for making and drinking coffee were common practice. Today we seem to need a reminder about how important it is to enjoy simple moments and to know traditional techniques. Dixon's set encourages us to slow down, take time to use

each object in the collection and focus on the process of brewing, instead of ordering another take-away at the closest café. With the *Brew* collection coffee can taste so much better. The milk pan has a 400 ml volume and is fitted with a long, straight handle, which is crucial for making use of it safely and comfortably. The pan is, hence, well balanced and easy to grip. As with other elements in the collection, it also has a sculptural look.

British designer Tom Dixon established his eponymous brand in 2002, as he says, to "re-think the product designer's relationship with industry". He works mainly in lighting, accessories and furniture. However, *Design Research Studio*, which is the label's interior architecture facility, founded in 2007, also designs innovative interiors and exteriors. Today, the globally celebrated designer with offices around the world can celebrate a range of 600 products, which are renowned for the finest quality materials and engineering techniques.

ROBIN HEATHER & KAI LINKE
Tiles for VIA , 2018 / VIA PLATTEN

Robin Heather and Kai Linke designed a series of geometrically-patterned cement tiles for VIA PLATTEN, a manufacturer specializing in floor tiles. Aiming at timeless designs and traditional handmade quality, the designers created a visually intriguing series drawing from the ornaments of the past. "Newly interpreted, it is reminiscent of old ornamentation and conveys a certain valence through longevity and patina." they say. These tiles of significant size 20 x 20 cm are covered with a geometric pattern that refers to classical ornament. "The asymmetry of a single tile allows the possibility to break up the regular layout just by a slight variation of array, creating surprising transitions and diverse situations in the overall picture." explain the designers. This playful idea transforms a flat floor into a dynamic field of optical illusion. Several options for arranging the pattern sequences allow the tiles to be laid differently within various interiors and to create an impression of movement between spaces: the surface does not look flat anymore, but seems to vibrate rhythmically. As the whole focus is on geometry, the design of the tiles is reduced to straight lines in two tones, which enhances the way the surface deceives our perception. Heather's and Linke's collection of tiles introduces a whimsical element into the interiors. The floor vibrates differently depending on where you stand and how you move across the space; as such, it can influence the character of the room. The bigger the surface, the stronger the effect.

Both designers, Robin Heather and Kai Linke, are

based in Frankfurt am Main in Germany. Heather runs a creative studio working in the areas of architecture, art and design. "We like to play the game of contrasts — contrasts of shape, material, colour and production methods." they state. And they produce their designs by fusing advanced digital technologies and traditional craftsmanship. Linke founded his studio in 2009 to develop lights and furniture as well as objects for public spaces or interior design. His portfolio is fueled by bold experiments with innovative forms, materials and also the way objects are manufactured. Drawing inspiration from everyday life, the designer examines different cultures.

PIETRO RUSSO
Wine Cooler A, 2017 / Editions Milano

Italian designer Pietro Russo was trained in painting and ceramics and then studied scenography. Between 1997 and 2001 he worked in Berlin in the field of set and interior design for film, but he also produced objects in limited editions. After his relocation to Milan at the turn of the millennium, he joined Lissoni Associati, where he worked on product and interior design for various brands. 2010 marked the establishment of his Milan-based atelier which he opened in order to continue the practice under his own name. Supported by a team of experts and a network of skilled Italian artisans, Russo is known to create objects that resonate with a particular space and its history. The official biography describes his approach to design in the following way: "Trusting his instinct, Pietro experiments tirelessly and is committed to long-lasting explorations of major topics such as science fiction, art and music seductions, sound, geometry, and the power of light in an endless attempt to transform

concepts and emotions, with his own hands, into one-of-a-kind objects and interiors designed like a real scenography."

For Editions Milano, a Milan-based manufacturer focusing on traditional techniques and collaborations with cutting-edge Italian designers, Russo created a collection of four beautiful wine coolers. Each consists of two parts mimicking the shape of a bottle. The top of each cooler has a sculpturally-shaped lid. Made of Arabescato and Marquinia marble, they have a brass glass inside, which allows the wine to be kept at the right temperature. Aiming to invent a device to chill wine that doesn't require ice, Russo used the natural properties of the noble material he selected. Marble's chilling abilities help to preserve the temperature of the bottle in the most natural way. As a result, the wine tastes great, and the coolers as objects look striking. The long lasting and precious marble makes the object an elegant accessory for every table. Each cooler has a different pattern inspired by geometric shapes, which alludes to ornaments in Italian churches and striped stone façades. To obtain such an excellent result the series is crafted by hand, by expert Italian craftsmen. Russo's wine coolers, produced in Italy, were a part of the debut collection of Editions Milano, which comprised furniture and objects designed by recognized designers.

#8

GOOD DESIGN IS THOROUGH
DOWN TO THE LAST DETAIL

"Nothing must be arbitrary
or left to chance. Care and
accuracy in the design process
show respect towards the user."

Dieter Rams

The design process for each product is complex and requires numerous professional skills. None of the stages is unessential, quite the contrary, each stage should be approached with the same attention and effort. "My heart belongs to the details." declares Dieter Rams. "I actually always found them to be more important than the big picture. Nothing works without details. They are everything, the baseline of quality." he adds. Apart from experimental projects, where leaving the final effect to chance can be necessary, all aspects of the design should be well thought out and accordingly well-executed. This attitude shows, as Rams states, the respect towards the user and also towards the materials and the specialists engaged in the process to realize the designer's vision. Attention to detail can determine the quality and define the unique character of an object.

LARA BOHINC
Collision Large Table Light, 2017

After graduating in industrial design from the Ljubljana Academy of Fine Arts, Lara Bohinc moved to London to complete her studies and specialize in metalwork and jewellery at the Royal College of Art. She eventually founded her studio in London in 1997, feeling encouraged by winning the British Fashion Council's New Generation Award. Ten years later, she opened her first store, also in London. Bohinc's practice has been from the outset multifaceted with the goal of bridging three design disciplines: jewellery, furniture, and objects. When designing, her aim is to create a combination of contrasts and look for bold yet light, graphic yet fluid and angular yet feminine forms. "While retaining a deep respect for the traditional principles of her craft, she has also drawn on her knowledge of industrial techniques and fused modernity of style with function to achieve a contemporary elegance." reads the official statement. Apart from creating her own stunning pieces, the designer has also worked as a design consultant for luxury brands in various sectors, among them Montblanc, Gucci and Cartier.

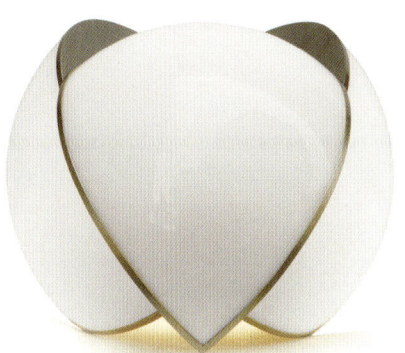

The Bohinc studio has introduced many unusually shaped light candleholders, vases, bowls as well as desk items and, since 2017, also lighting. The *Collision* Light collection is the first one featuring lamps in the designer's portfolio, and yet another captivating expression of the designer's obsession with deconstruction and reconfiguration of pure geometric forms. The *Collision* series consists of a variation on broken orbs and a motif Bohinc primarily explored in her jewellery. The composition is an intriguing arrangement of four identical quarter-spheres colliding or breaking out from one sphere, depending on the way one perceives it. Each quarter of the orb functions as an individual source of light. "*Collision* is about the splitting of perfection; in this case a perfect sphere has broken but in a very symmetrical manner. It is almost like the pieces are sliding apart and could easily slide back." said the designer. Indeed, the way the geometric form is deconstructed gives a dynamic feeling even when the lamp is not in use. Manufactured in Italy, the framework is made of metal, the domes are acrylic. Interestingly, the table lamp is not equipped with any base, it just lies on the surface, enhancing the visual effect. The collection includes two table lamps in various sizes, and a ceiling lamp.

THOMAS BENTZEN
Mingle Cushion, 2012 / Muuto

Industrial designer Thomas Bentzen is a graduate of the Royal Danish Academy of Fine Arts — School of Design. Since 2010, when he established his own studio in Copenhagen, the designer has been creating products for everyday life, which could be characterized by their simplicity, rationality and functionality. Design, according to Bentzen, should engage and awake curiosity. The main objective in exploring materials and forms for new designs is their enduring aspect. In order to create long-lasting objects, the designer gained extensive knowledge of materials, in addition, he also studied both craftsmanship and industrial manufacturing processes. His style is very clean and precise. Elegantly playing with geometrical forms, Benzten invents shapes that are unconventional, fresh and elegant. His collaboration with Muuto, a manufacturer dedicated to the promotion of Scandinavian design, was particularly fruitful. Between 2011 and 2013, the designer worked as design manager, and from 2013 to 2015, he was the brand's head of design. The *Mingle cushion* is one of the projects he developed for Muuto.

"My idea was to create a cushion series based on the simple mingling of textile and colour. The process was straightforward, yet at the same time complex." comments the designer. "It turned out to be an exciting journey through colour and texture and in the end, we found colours and textiles that complemented each other and mingled well with one another." he adds. Created for mingling with each other on the sofa, the *Mingle* collection is made of two different textiles from the textile manufacturer Kvadrat (Coda and Steelcut). The contrasting colours and textures are combined in a way that enhances the refined quality of the fabrics and their rich colours. The *Mingle* collection is made to be touched and not simply to sit on the sofa or armchair. Bentzen's selections of the palette and composition entice the user to interact. The cushion comes in two shapes: rectangular — 60 x 40 cm; and square — 50 x 50 cm. Given the diversity of complementing hues and their tactile qualities, they look great but are also pleasing to the touch. Last but not least, Bentzen designed cushions that will last for a long time.

DOSHI LEVIEN
Raas and Lila Fabrics, 2018 / Kvadrat

Kvadrat has been manufacturing exceptional fabrics since 1968. Embracing innovative techniques and teaming up with the most creative designers of the time, the brand pushes the boundaries of aesthetics. Their high-quality textiles are used for upholsteries, window coverings, plus rugs and home accessories. The highly talented designer-duo Doshi Levien is among the design studios collaborating with Kvadrat. The London-based design practice, founded by Jonathan Levien and Nipa Doshi in 2000, gained international acclaim for their ingenious way of bringing together many worlds in their designs. While working across disciplines and industries, they celebrate the hybrid and explore the fusion of cultures, technologies, industrial design and fine craftsmanship. Their work includes industrial products ranging from furniture to ceramics as well as installations and objects in limited editions. For Kvadrat, Doshi Levien designed two textile collections inspired by a mix of contrasting inspirations, including royal Indian miniature paintings, glazed Chinese ceramics and Modernist paintings. The result is stunning, as the sensual fabrics are a great combination of unique textures and vibrant yet subtle colours.

The duo first mixed and painted more than 100 gouache colours by hand to create a palette that was later used during the production to dye the yarn. The effect of this process is unique, as the hues of the *Lila* and *Raas* collections cannot be found in any existing colour system. The intriguing surface, independent from the colour, delights the eyes while not creating the obvious. Used as upholstery on any piece of furniture, it will create an exceptionally nuanced visual effect that is lively and eye-catching. A tactile, bouclé-like feel that is very tactile is the result of combining two voluminous unicoloured yarns: a regular yarn in the weft and an irregularly textured slub yarn in the warp. While *Raas* is densely woven and has a more precise grid, *Lila*'s striated pattern has a more relaxed character. The names of the fabrics are derived from Hindu mythology — *Lila* means "play" or "dance" and *Raas* refers to "aesthetics" and "feeling". "There is play of aesthetics, between ancient and modern references, vivid and faded colours, memories and remains of colour on architecture; two colours layered on top of each other like textured glazes." notes the duo. Both fabrics are made of 92% new wool and 8% of nylon, are 140 centimetres wide, come in 29 colourways and are very durable.

ANNE BOYSEN
Toward, 2012-2015 / Erik Jørgensen

 Manufactured by Erik Jørgensen, *Toward* is a refined, and creative combination of sofa, armchair and daybed. It consists of a simple, flat mattress base and two backrests of different sizes and shapes. Additionally, the designer has created two cushions that are loose and can be placed interchangeably depending on the user's needs. "I wanted to make a piece of furniture that allowed users to relax in as many different ways as possible." explains Boysen. This constellation not only gives the user a freedom to employ the sofa in numerous ways, but also contributes to its original look. The proportions between each of its parts and the smoothly rounded edges add a touch of sophistication to this unique sofa. While creating the design for the Danish manufacturer, Anne Boysen was fascinated by the monochromatic trend in furniture design. *Toward* was designed in 2012, manufactured one year later, and had a colour update in 2015. Since then it has been available in six colour variants that combine shades of green, dark blue, pink and brown as well as light grey and dark grey. Each variant is made of six different Kvadrat fabrics. Every element of the sofa has a different hue, and the whole works together as it has been thoroughly thought through by the designer. The nuances of hue and the various upholsteries work perfectly with the different shapes, while the seamless quality celebrates the craftsmanship.

Anne Boysen is a Danish architect and designer who has run her own studio in the outskirts of Copenhagen since 2012. This multifaceted practice spans design, art and architecture. Her furniture is as much functional as driven by aesthetic values. They are characterised by sophisticated compositions and harmonious proportions, even if experimental in form (especially challenging geometry). The result is visually striking. For the designer, colour plays a crucial role, hence her designs employ expressive and rich hues. The refined quality of Boysen's designs is an effect of her attention to detail at every single stage of the product's development. "After several years maintaining the pace of the trend-oriented design industry, she now listens to her gut feeling, increasingly moving in a more reflective, artistic direction with an emphasis on aesthetically sustainable projects with longer deadlines: more passion, impeccable skill and, above all, silence." emphasizes Henriette Noermark in the designer's biographical note.

SCHOLTEN & BAIJINGS
Paper Porcelain, 2010 / HAY

The *Paper Porcelain* collection of tableware, which looks very much like coarse recycled paper, is actually crafted of porcelain. The ceramic's speckled appearance plays with the user's perception. At first glance, the surface of the pieces is matt, but after a closer inspection, one can notice tiny iron specks in the porcelain, which are supposed to resemble the quality of recycled paper. Designed by the Dutch design duo Scholten & Baijings, the collection was initially created for an exhibition. Based on a paper model and realized in specially developed porcelain, the ability to imitate paper's structure, thereby deceiving the eye, was possible and the set went into regular production. Producing the pieces was quite challenging, as the porcelain has to be very thin to emulate paper, but, at the same time, it should not break easily. The collection is made durable thanks to the selection of strong solid stones that are then crushed and water added to make the clay. The choice of stone also contributes to getting the right colour. The lines on the surface of the mould are modified by hand before it is put into the oven. Then, the potters use a special machine to polish the surface layers. The whole series comprises an espresso and a coffee cup, both with saucers, a mug, and a tea plate. This exceptional service in porcelain is manufactured in Arita, Japan, for HAY. The brand also collaborated with the duo on a wide selection of furniture, textiles and accessories.

  Stefan Scholten and Carole Baijings established their multifaceted design studio back in 2000. The Amsterdam-based duo works across furniture, lighting, glassware, textile, graphic and exhibition design. Drawing inspiration from art and design history, they always look to create objects that could reinvent the way we live and work. Scholten graduated from the Design Academy Eindhoven, and within the practice he is responsible for the ideology. Baijings, a self-taught designer, focuses on design detail and production. Perfectionism in their use of patterns, hues and graphic elements is at the core of their creative work. A successful design, according to Scholten & Baijings, is one that the users can enjoy for a long time.

ALDO BAKKER
Facet Bottle Stopper, 2017 / Atelier Swarovski Home

"The pieces encapsulate Bakker's fixation with a purity of form and materiality, achieving the perfect balance of function and beauty" - this is what Atelier Swarovski says about the brand's collaboration with the Dutch designer Aldo Bakker. The *Facet* collection is a set of four bottle stoppers cut from a single piece of Swarovski crystal, each in a different hue. The bottle stoppers are divided into two parts. The longitudinal bottom is clear and smooth, which contrasts with the much more complex structure of the upper part of the stopper. Crystal is cut very precisely to catch the light, and play with it to create captivating visual effects. The multifaceted top is easy to grasp, which is essential given the object's function and the qualities of crystal. As in his other collaborations with Atelier Swarovski, Bakker succeeded in creating an object with extremely elegant, light, and radiant forms. The choice of hues is another striking component. In addition to clear crystal, *Facet* comes in black diamond, light sapphire and jonquil, each enhancing the spectacle of light. Although the designer's

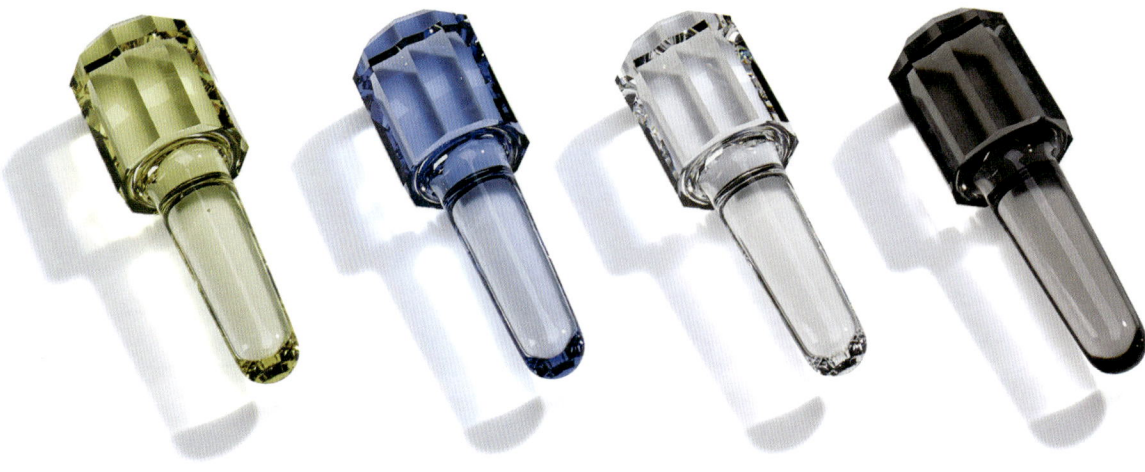

stoppers are meant for any bottle, their sophisticated form makes them the ideal companion to a bottle of champagne. The collection achieves the perfect balance of function and beauty.

Bakker's educational background is non-traditional. He was first trained as a silversmith, working on commission, and then moved into furniture and product design. He established his own practice in 1994, and since then has developed a very distinctive and imaginative visual language. Unlike many designers, Bakker does not approach a design as solving a practical problem. Functionality is an aspect that is considered at a later stage of the process. The objects he creates nearly always originate from fascination with a form. Inspired by everything around him, Bakker sketches what he observes and finds interesting before examining whether a particular form can be transformed into a new object. At the same time, the designer challenges the traditional ways we use objects to create practical, yet original, and playful designs.

TADAO ANDO
Ando Time, 2015 / Venini

An hourglass is not an obvious design object, and yet it fascinates many designers with its poetic potential. Japanese architect Tadao Ando created this one in 2011 for the Murano-based, iconic glass manufacturer, VENINI. The brand, established by Paolo Venini in 1921, is famous for working with some of the most celebrated designers and architects. All of the manufacturer's projects are spectacular, but the *Ando Time* clearly stands out. VENINI's laboratory continues to develop new specimens of glass, challenging traditional techniques, and thus producing numerous objects that pay tribute to the beauty of glass art. "The collaboration between the master craftsmanship of the Venetian Glass and the layered geometric form has created this special piece of object", notes Ando. "Architecture is defined through 'Space' and 'Time'. Perhaps metaphorically an hourglass can denote architecture. The flow of the sand carries along the thoughts of the past and the future." he adds. Ando's hourglass has a complex geometric form consisting of two main elements: the outside shell is a twisted glass prism with a triangular base on both ends, while the inside piece forms a glass cylinder of two parts in different colours. The latter holds sand, which passes from one part to the other through a titanium connection. This structure required a special cast-iron mould and a complex engineering process. Its sculptural appearance delights the viewer with its proportions, sharp edges, expressive curves and use of colours enhancing the play of light. Ando's hourglass makes us wish time to pass, as it is an aesthetic pleasure to observe the transition of the sand.

Self-taught in architecture, former boxer and truck driver, Tadao Ando, is one of the most celebrated architects in the world. Renowned for his minimal and cast-in-place concrete buildings, he established his Osaka-based practice, Tadao Ando Architects and Associates, in 1968. Inspired by architects like Le Corbusier, Ludwig Mies Van der Rohe, Frank Lloyd Wright and Louis Kahn, he developed a unique and highly recognizable style of his own. Ando's buildings realized around the

globe are remarkable structures as well as sensational experiences, with aesthetics inspired by Japanese culture. Product design is a small but very interesting part of Ando's practice.

SOVRAPPENSIERO DESIGN STUDIO
Radiant Wallpaper, 2016 / Texturae

Sovrappensiero Design Studio, the result of creative collaboration between Lorenzo De Rosa and Ernesto Iadevia, was established in Milan in 2007. The duo of Italian designers has a resolutely unconventional approach to design. Whether they develop a lamp, a vase or a grinder, their experimental research leads to surprising and innovative forms. Working in both industrial production and limited editions, Sovrappensiero offers, at the same time, a dream-like aesthetic vision and perfectly functional objects. Playing mainly with shapes and combinations of materials, the designers often challenge our expectations. Their designs are as sophisticated as they are delicate in expression. Texturae is a brand created in 2016 to revolutionize the world of wallpapers. Their idea, successfully realized, was to gather innovative artistic visions and, with the help of advanced technology, create original graphics for decorating spaces. Their portfolio is truly inspirational, full of elegance, sophistication and one-of-a-kind ideas. Texturae has reinvented wallpaper and thus transformed the environments where we live, work and function.

Sovrappensiero and Texturae teamed up to create the Warp collection, which is described by the manufacturer as follows: "Bold colours, extreme overlapping shapes that become icons, perspectives that go on forever. The Warp collection has a personality that does not go unnoticed." The studio's contribution to the series is the *Radiant* wallpaper, which employs a graphic motif of radiating lines. It is available in several colour options, including black, white, grey and ochre. However, the optical illusion effect is most visible against darker hues. The pattern is made up of lines that balance between rhythmical repetitions and interruptions of the regular flow. It likes a musical composition that changes tempo, has its own crescendos and diminuendos. The tune is played here on the surface of the wall and effectively resonates in the space. A close observation of the wallpaper shows tiny details in the pattern, which from further away look like accents on a blurred surface. Like all wallpapers from Texturae, *Radiant* has transformative abilities and embraces the interior with intriguing patterns that play with the flatness of the walls to create three-dimensional impressions.

ELISA STROZYK
Wooden Textiles, 2014-now

Born and based in Berlin, Elisa Strozyk studied textile and surface design at the KHB in Berlin. She also studied design at the École Nationale Supérieure des Arts Décoratifs (ENSAD) in Paris and graduated in Future Textile Design at Central Saint Martins in London. 2009 marked her return to Berlin and the opening of her own studio focusing on designing furniture, lighting and textiles. Strozyk gained recognition for her bold experiments with materials that challenged their traditional qualities. One of her most fascinating projects is the ongoing *Wooden Textiles* series (started in 2014), in which Strozyk transformed pieces of wood into malleable surfaces to attach them to textile bases. The new material, something between wood and textile becomes, a sculptural version of a table-runner, a rug, or, as presented, here a curtain.

Strozyk was commissioned by Coordination Berlin to design a wooden backdrop for the Technogels flagship store, an outlet selling high-end gel mattresses and pillows in Berlin. The curtain is made of hand-dyed maple wood and was created similarly to other textiles from the collection, first by deconstructing wood into small geometrical pieces and assembling them onto a textile base. "Depending on the geometry and size of the tiles, each design shows a different behaviour regarding flexibility and mobility." explains the designer. The main goal is to convey a tactile experience and to challenge assumptions with the playful use of the wood, a material usually associated with solidity. Strozyk exploits the public's curiosity about the new character of the wooden surface, which is between hard and soft, teasing our senses and what we are used to expecting from the material. "It looks and smells familiar, but feels strange, as it is able to move and form in unexpected ways." she says. A curtain is often touched and moved, so the idea of a wooden textile is the most interesting choice of material. Mixing wood with fabric is visually striking, especially as the wood can be also dyed to enhance its three-dimensional effects. The innovative, sculptural window decoration looks different each time it is set in motion.

CRISTINA CELESTINO
Profumo, 2016 / Ichendorf Milano

After graduating in architecture from Iuav in Venice, Cristina Celestino worked with numerous architectural studios. She gradually decided to focus on interior architecture and design and relocated to Milan in 2009 to establish her own brand, Attico Design, specializing in lamps and furniture. Since then, Celestino has developed objects for design labels, and has created limited editions for design galleries. Celestino has also worked as a creative director for luxury brands, and due to her architectural background, she is engaged in interior and exhibition projects. "As a great collector of Italian design masterpieces and being curious towards all objects, she bases her work on observation and research, plumbing the potential of shapes, functions and going beyond the traditional relations between fashion, art and design and embeds a passionate interest for the old and the new, the traditional and the contemporary in her projects, and also she develops creative solutions and freely plays with ideas." states Celestino's philosophy, which is reflected in her extraordinary products.

Profumo is an essence dispenser made of blown candle borosilicate glass. It is clearly divided into two contrasting elements. The cylinder is made of the ribbed glass, which results in a complex texture, in a play of light as well as in a dded depth. On its top, there is a sectioned sphere, which the designer describes as "reminiscent of the corolla in which drive for a better experience of perfumes is a deliberate homage to master perfumers' ampoules". Both elements enhance each other in an alluring way. Celestino's designs are characterized by a great sense for materials, by their unusual textures, and by their shapes. Celestino's deep research results in ingenious and aesthetic objects, which, like the *Profumo*, are made to fulfil their functions perfectly. As envisioned by the designer, this sophisticated essence dispenser does speak the language of perfume. The manufacturer of *Profumo* is a glass-making specialist founded in the early 20th century in Ichendorf and relocated to Milan in the 1990s. Famous for precious ornaments, the brand evolved its style in the 1950s to favour clean shapes and a purity of materials. Today, the company collaborates with leading Italian designers and produces state-of-the-art glass tableware fusing tradition and innovation, ancient techniques and modern shapes, in order to create unique objects.

#9

GOOD DESIGN IS
ENVIRONMENTALLY-FRIENDLY

"Design makes an
important contribution
to the preservation of the
environment. It conserves
resources and minimizes the
physical and visual pollution
throughout the lifecycle of
the product."

Dieter Rams

Some predictions warn that there will be more plastic waste than fish in the world's oceans by 2050. Given the culture of overproduction and waste, this and many other environmental disasters could happen much more quickly. Improving our environment is now one of the main challenges for designers. The emphasis is clearly on sustainable solutions, innovative materials, and ways to reduce pollution. Preserving the planet is an objective to which all contemporary designers are invited to contribute. By challenging the boundaries of technologies, favouring renewable sources of energy, recycling or using natural components they can bring innovative responses to re-creating the world in an eco-friendly mode. In the wake of the disquieting scale of consumption and pollution, addressing the use of materials seems fundamental. The lifecycle of each product should be as close to nature as possible.

JIN JURAMOTO
Jin Chair, 2017 / Offecct

Jin Kuramoto's design for Swedish manufacturer Offecct is a 100% biological chair. "Many of my ideas are born when I make prototypes and I believe that you can only find new values in design by doing so and using your hands. While working on a paper model of a chair, I found myself arriving at a new structure which became the starting point for *Jin*." says the designer. The innovative structure of the chair is made using flax fibre. It is a tested biological material that proved to be successfully industrialized and can be used to produce sustainable furniture. To create the body of *Jin*, thin layers of flax fibres were placed atop each other. They have formed the chair's strong shell, while the inside of the structure is empty. Thanks to this ingenious system, *Jin* is not only ecological, but is also ultralight. Neither the environmentally-friendly process used nor the chair's minimalist aesthetics reduces the comfort of sitting. To make it even more comfortable, it can be upholstered. *Jin* is also available in carbon-fibre.

Kuramoto's design exemplifies the Swedish manufacturer's "Lifecircle" philosophy of minimizing the production's impact on the environment. "We aim to use as few of the Earth's resources as possible in our production, and also to take care of the products we have made through circular recycling", according to their statement. The brand's collection is created according to the needs of the market, but developing solutions that prolong their products' lifecycle to make them sustainable in the long term is at the heart of each design and production process. Offecct's engineers and commissioned designers work closely together to explore new possibilities and find sustainable solutions for the furniture industry of tomorrow. Interestingly, the label introduced a second-hand market for their own products to enable customers to replace or renovate their furnishings.

Jin Kuramoto graduated from Kanazawa College of Art in 1999 and founded his Tokyo-based studio in 2008. The designer develops furniture, home electronics and accessories. Kuramoto describes his approach to design as introducing the essence of things, which he does with a very clear and innovative style.

ATELIER MENDINI
Alex Chaise Longue, 2017 / ecopixel®

Ecopixel is an Italian brand co-created by a manufacturer, Claudio Milioto, and a designer, Juan Puylaert, around the concept of never-ending recyclability. "We should see products as a precise amount of material that can be re-used for something else." they stress. They call their own productions the "in-between moments of material-solidification". Ecopixel's philosophy is based on the principle of reducing waste, particularly plastic, also by modifying the design of new products to effectively minimize the waste their production generates.

"*Alex*, my Chaise Longue, looking at Impressionism", as Alessandro Mendini calls his design, is the result of the brand's collaboration with the iconic Italian and international designer. This remarkable piece, using innovative techniques, transforms polyethylene waste (shredded plastic, to be precise) into a pointillist design object, which can just as easily be seen as a work of art. Expressive both in its texture and choice of colours, the chaise longue's shape derives from the combination of polygonal plane surfaces with live edge lines, which results in a powerful, origami-like form that, nevertheless, offers great comfort. The dynamic character of *Alex*'s

shape is enhanced by the play of colourful pixels which are randomly combined. The eight vivid hues have been carefully selected by Mendini himself. Creating such an innovative and spectacular piece of outdoor furniture was possible thanks to ecopixel's special, pressurized rotational production method. "The remarkable qualities of ecopixel have been an opportunity for powerful expression through texture and colour." praised the designer. The design is 100% recyclable and incredibly durable. *Alex* is a limited-edition product by Alessandro Mendini, Francesco Mendini and Alex Mocika of Atelier Mendini. Alessandro established the latter together with his brother Francesco in 1989. It is based in Milan and works across disciplines as it gathers architects, graphic and industrial designers. The studio is famous for deep research and bold experimentations with materials. They even dedicated a special department to develop this aspect of their practice. Alessandro Mendini graduated in architecture from the Politecnico di Milano, and his career as a designer and architect is characterized by a fusion of various influences and diverse forms.

SUPER LOCAL
Trending Terrazzo, 2017

Dutch designers, Pim van Baarsen and Luc van Hoeckel, created Super Local to design products, offer services and systems to improve the quality of life of the poor. "We are passionate problem solvers, story tellers and fixers, and our human-centred approach is hands-on and based on collaboration with local communities, organizations and partners." they declare. One of the projects they participated was realized in Zanzibar and used waste glass to create a very special homewares collection. The journey started two years earlier, when Super Local, as part of a group of designers, visited Zanzibar and were shocked to learn that huge numbers of discarded glass bottles left by crowds of tourists visiting the African island were actually not being recycled. Commissioned by *bottle up*, the designers came up with the idea to invite local craftsmen to an eco-friendly collaboration and to create products using the glass bottles from hotels and resorts.

The initiators of the *bottle up* project demonstrating that glass does not necessarily have to be wasted, was *bottle up foundation* established by Hubert and Elisabeth van Doorne as a reaction to huge amount of waste they found on Zanzibar. They commissioned a group of designers via Dutch Design Foundation to research solutions. The second part of the project was

Trending Terrazzo, when Super Local worked together with OSΔOOS and Klaas Kuiken. Van Baarsen explains that "It's hard to create nice products using broken or dirty glass. That's how we eventually came up with *Terrazzo*, which we made by mixing glass shards with cement." Glass waste transformed into highly aesthetic objects has resulted in stunning new products. The *Terrazzo* homeware collection delights the eye with its gleaming, multicolour structure, which beautifully contrasts with the solid forms and geometric shapes of the objects. The whole series consists of a bench, a table, a dish and a vase and is exclusively produced and sold in Zanzibar. The idea not only recycles the material, but also makes something that could be used by local tourist resorts and increases a sense of the value of recycling. The essential was to engage local craftsmen instead of importing objects or furniture. Currently, most hotels and resorts import their furniture form Asia, mostly Bali, because of the lack of well-crafted products on Zanzibar itself and because it is relatively cheap.

ADIDAS DESIGN TEAM
3D-printed Ocean Plastic Shoe, 2015

    The amount of plastic trash dumped in the oceans is estimated at 8 million metric tons per year, which means that a garbage truck full of plastic is thrown into the oceans every single minute. Unbelievable as it may sound, the predictions say that, in terms of weight, there will be more plastic in the oceans than fish by 2050, and the numbers are constantly growing. Inventing solutions to recycle the existing plastic waste seems especially crucial, particularly now that more and more ocean clean-up initiatives have been undertaken, including building special devices to collect some of the plastic islands floating on the surface of the waters. Many manufacturers have developed ways to re-use the material and make new products from it. One of them was launched by Adidas and the idea was to design a new sneaker with an upper part made from ocean plastic content and a 3D-printed midsole made of recycled polyester and gill nets. The company declares that reducing their carbon footprint, as well as their use of virgin plastic, is a fundamental goal for their production.

This innovative model was initiated in collaboration with *Parley for the Oceans*, an organization aimed at raising awareness of the fragility of the oceans and alerting people about the current situation. Parley is a platform for environmental projects that can help to reverse the oceans' destruction. Together with Adidas, they work on new technologies and innovative footwear. The manufacturer initially created new sustainable materials used in products for athletes. The 3D-printed *Ocean Plastic sneaker* was the first step torward leading to more global solutions that could effectively reduce plastic waste in oceans. A couple of years later, Adidas offered a couple of models created with yarn made in collaboration with *Parley for the Oceans*. "Some of the yarn features Parley Ocean Plastic™ which is made of recycled waste, intercepted from beaches and coastal communities before it reaches the ocean." states the producer. The most innovative shoes have an in-built NFC chip, which after scanning with a mobile phone, allows the wearer to follow the story of the shoe from plastic bottle to final product, and provides additional information about how to help to protect the oceans.

MARJAN VAN AUBEL
Current Window, 2016 / Caventou

Dutch designer Marjan van Aubel graduated from the Royal College of Art and the Rietveld Academy Design LAB. Her practice is highly innovative and focuses on exploring the interconnections between sustainability, design and technology. The results of her research are both fascinating and revolutionary. As a part of numerous collaborations with scientists, engineers, and institutions such as Swarovski and the Dutch Energy Centre, van Aubel has developed new ways to promote extreme energy efficiency through intelligent design. Her signature idea is to integrate solar cells into various objects, which mimic the process of photosynthesis, as we know it from plants, to generate energy. Objects in van Aubel's portfolio are not merely objects, they always have an added value. Van Aubel also co-founded an award-wining, sustainable design collective, Caventou, which focuses on re-defining solar technology to make it a part of everyday life.

Current Window uses the latest solar cell technology. Integrated into the window glass, the technology efficiently generates electricity from daylight. "Its dye-sensitive solar cells work much like the process of photosynthesis, turning the properties of colour into an electrical current for devices and appliances." explains the designer. Different hues have variable wavelengths, hence generating more or less energy. Van Aubel works closely with the dye-solar cell manufacturers when creating the window pattern to make best use of its potential, and still achieve a beautiful visual effect. The system is scalable, so when covering more surface area, it generates more energy, and it is flexible enough to be adjusted to individual needs. The practical aspect of the *Current Window* does not diminish its aesthetic appeal. The solar cells not only are coloured, but can also form various patterns to decorate the windows and even, due to the shaded structure, provide some privacy. The designer calls the technique a modern version of stained glass. Marjan van Aubel used the same technology to design a table, which becomes an innovative piece of furniture. Solar cells in the surface of the *Current Table* enable it to harvest energy indoors to charge devices via a USB port. No cables are needed and the process works even under diffused light. Last but not least, a specially developed app allows the intensity of the light to be checked as well as the level of stored energy.

DOTE
Accessories for Pets, 2017

Dote was founded in 2017 by two furniture designers, Nic Wallenberg and Helena Hedestedt. It is a London-based pet design studio dedicated to creating consciously crafted objects for pets and their owners. As the saying goes, need is the mother of invention. Dote was born as a remedy for the lack of smart, modern and sustainable essentials that the designers couldn't find for their two cats, Sika and Kira. They decided to fill the gap and to launch their own label. The first collection of prototypes includes: an inventive *Modular Wall Climber*, which effectively increases any indoor surface even in very restricted spaces, and works as a minimalistic decoration for the wall; the *Grooming Set* consists of a silicon brush and a recycled stainless steel comb; an elegant *Carrier* designed to safely transport small animals with shoulder straps and a soft mesh lining; the *Mouldable Blanket* that can be easily sculpted and makes a perfect playground; and toys from the production off-cuts. As pet accessories are usually poorly produced out of cheap and flimsy materials, or with no sense for aesthetics (or both), the duo's main objective is to offer well-crafted, and simple objects, which would be aesthetically pleasing, compatible with various interiors and meet the practical need of pets.

"Dote believes that each and every piece should be environmentally responsible, enhance a space and, most importantly, encourage harmonious co-habitation." the duo emphasizes. Their aspiration is to create objects that are completely sustainable. Crafted primarily in strictly regulated Swedish factories, Dote's products are all vegan and from partly recycled and fully recyclable PET felt, which is made from recycled plastic bottles. "We have chosen to work with felt because of its versatility, durability and a pet's natural attraction to the material due to its heat insulating qualities. The combination of durability with the felt's porous structure makes it particularly suited to a cat's needs." says Hedestedt. Scratching and climbing actually lowers the pets' stress level and is helpful in manicuring the claws. The thermal and acoustic properties of the felt, which insulates and absorbs noises, should not be underestimated, either.

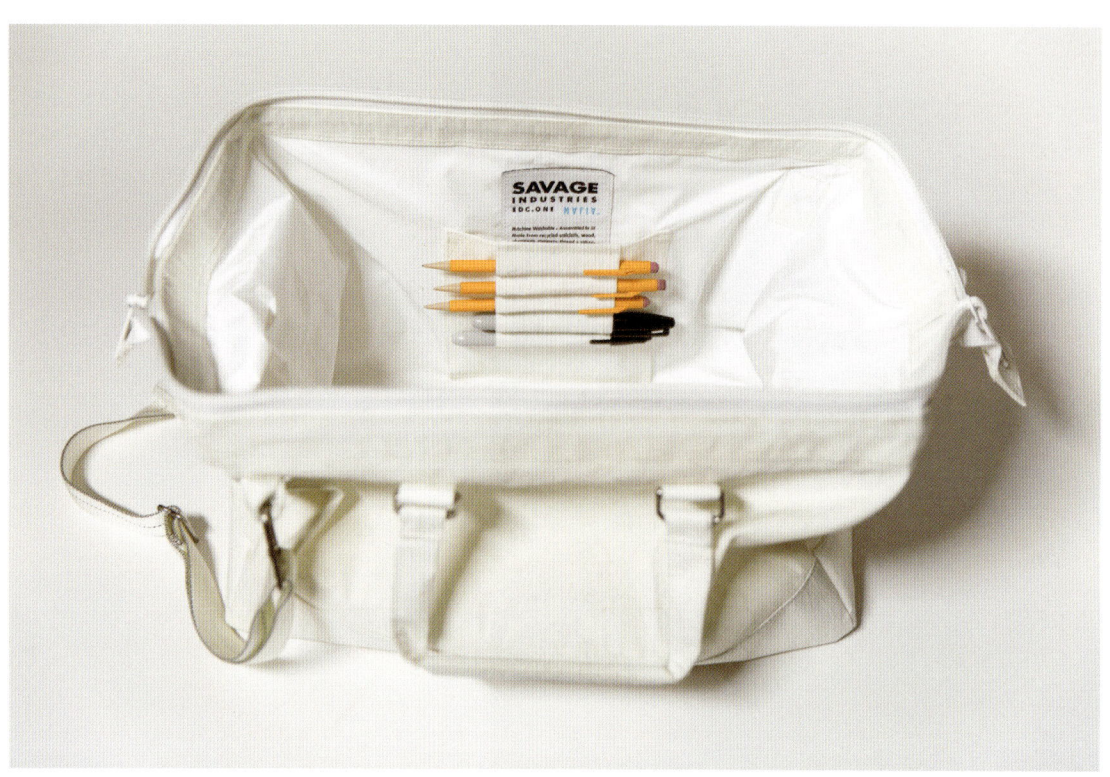

ADAM SAVAGE
EDC One, 2017 / MAFIA Bags

"When you get a MAFIA bag, you're also get a piece of the ocean and supporting the local community and the sustainable practices." say brother-and-sister duo Marcos and Paz Mafia, who launched their brand MAFIA in 2012 in their hometown of Buenos Aires (two years later they moved the headquarters to San Francisco). Their passion for nautical sports (Marcos used to be a professional kite-surfer) and interest in sustainability provided plenty of inspiration for creating an upcycled bag manufacturing company. The bags are produced from recycled sails donated directly to the company by athletes, organizations or individuals. Each of their designs is a unique piece. In addition to a wide range of basic models, MAFIA Bags has initiated several collaborations with designers to create special projects.

Together with Adam Savage, a former editor-in-chief at Tested.com, they created a NASA-inspired everyday carry bag, the *EDC One*. "I kept it simple, and focused on access to contents and durability. The colour is chosen because I love NASA, but more importantly because all other tool bags are dark and that is wrong. I've spent too long for being unable to find things at the bottom of my tool bags. This ends now." comments Savage. The bag is durable (or even indestructible, as promised by the manufacturers, who offer a lifetime warranty) and lightweight. Another practical solution is that it comes with a strap. The handles are innovatively held together with magnets. The shape was influenced by various iconic bags and toolboxes, but it mainly draws from Neil Armstrong's stowage bag, which he took to the moon to store Apollo's hardware in. The clamshell mouth is supported by a wide steel spring that holds its shape and makes the bag much easier to use. Inside, there is also a handy pencil pocket. A smaller version of the bag, the *EDC Two* is also available in white. As they are manufactured primarily from upcycled and salvaged sailcloth, every bag is unique and hence identified with a hand-written serial number indicating the model and production number.

KARIM RASHID
Bobble®, 2016 / bobble

Bobble is on a mission to "eliminate the outrageous waste of single-serve disposable beverages by creating reusable drinking solutions that you actually want to carry all day long", the company states. Their bottle is reusable and resilient while looking chic. The bottles are sleek and easy to hold. By encouraging health and fitness (it is important to hydrate one's body while exercising or during a hectic day), they effectively reduce single-serve waste. *Bobble* is a stylish accessory for contemporary life. It is designed by one of the most prolific minds among contemporary designers, Egyptian-born, Canadian-raised and New York-based, Karim Rashid. His style, full of fantasy and vivid colours, finds innovative expression in fields such as furniture, tableware, lighting and packaging to name but a few. Rashid's designs are striking in their originality and pleasing forms and in masterfully selected palettes of colour. "I believe that we could be living in an entirely different world — one that is full of real contemporary inspiring objects, spaces, places, worlds, spirits and experiences." reads the designer's manifesto. Rashid's playful and exuberant designs are certainly a positive inspiration in our everyday lives.

Bobble is yet another of his designs which, while being functional, is also inventive and aesthetically pleasing. The bottle is equipped with a portable carbon filter for the *Classic, Infuse* and *Sport* versions, and with a micro filter for the *Presse*, a great innovation that makes filtration on-the-go possible. As the system removes chlorine and organic contaminants from the tap water, the filtered liquid is clean and crisp. No need to buy another disposable plastic bottle, *bobble* can always be refilled and produce filtered water at any time and place, with a quality guaranty. A single *bobble* filter can replace at least 300 normal water bottles, which means that its positive environmental impact is significant. "The brilliance of *bobble* is that it is totally universal, meeting global consumer needs — staying hydrated, saving money and the planet, and great design." says Rashid. The designer's signature use of colours gives *bobble* a lively accent: the filter, the cap and a small handle come in green, red, blue, magenta, black or yellow. The sinusoid shape of the bottle makes it easy to grasp.

BRIAN SIRONI
BIT Radiator, 2013 / antoniolupi

      Can a radiator be sustainable? Brian Sironi's *BIT*, manufactured by Antonio Lupi, is the ultimate, positive answer to this question. Made of aluminium, this vertical radiator has an unexpectedly minimal form. Its monolithic shape gives a discrete, yet decorative touch to any bathroom. "Small changes make a difference. The surface of *BIT* is marked by a sequence of vertical bands generated by small dimensional variations." explains Sironi. The irregular arrangement of the vertical slats creates a graphic yet tactile visual effect. "*BIT* 'draws' the wall to a rhythmic sequence of lights and shadows generated by slight variations of the surface, by alternating recesses and protrusions...a heat origami." as the manufacturer describes the design. Flat, yet far from boring with a surface that can effectively warm up a bathroom, it is available in various lengths. More importantly, it is produced from 100 % recycled aluminium, thus fully sustainable. The manufacturer supplied *BIT* with a primer that can be painted over to personalize the design according to the user's need, something that could be very convenient when re-decorating a bathroom. The radiator can become one with the wall if painted in the same hue, or be in stark contrast to emphasize its pure

shape. A lighter version of *BIT* was also released in 2014, with a 7-centimetre-thickness, which complements the minimal body. It is available in both water and electrical versions. Electronics integrated into the radiator allow it to be managed with a remote control.

Brian Sironi graduated in industrial design from Politecnico di Milano. After being trained in the USA, he established his own studio, which is based in Milan. The Italian designer's goal is to combine an industrial design approach with handicraft culture. His designs explore pure and minimalistic shapes. Antoniolupi is a brand that has been specializing in bathroom furniture for several decades. Creativity, innovation and style are at the core of their 100 % made-in-Italy products. Their minimalist aesthetics results in beautiful bathroom equipment that is highly innovative and of great quality.

RYAN MARIO YASIN
Petit Pli Clothing, 2017

Ryan Mario Yasin invented a truly revolutionary fabric, which allows clothes to grow along with the child. Finding children's clothes on the market dull and ill fitting, Yasin launched his London-based brand to offer a highly innovative solution that combined technology and fashion. His niece and nephew, Ronja and Viggo, were his biggest inspirations. Trained as an aeronautic engineer specializing in deployable structures, he used the most advanced technology for his amazing collection. Resembling origami, the clothes have been designed to be versatile, on and off the body. Dedicated for young children between 4 and 36 months, they are made of bi-directionally expanding fabric, which can accommodate up to seven sizes as children grow in their first two years. "*Petit Pli*'s versatile, waterproof shells are pleated in such a way that they can grow bi-directionally to custom-fit a range of sizes. The continuous size adjustment is a new way of approaching garment design, one suitable to high growth rates and discrepancies in children's sizes." states the brand. Visually effective, thanks to the special pleating process, the material is indeed flexible enough to adjust while being really hard wearing. The result improves not only parent's clothing bills, but also the environment by leading to significant waste reduction. By expanding up to seven sizes, it equates to seven times less waste than traditional garments that would need to be replaced as the child grew. The fabric they currently use for production is synthetic, and although using less of the material contributes hugely to slow down plastic consumption, they keep researching to find alternative materials. The company also continues to develop its range of products.

One of huge advantages of the *Petit Pli* clothes is that they are ultra-lightweight and very easy to fold, so they require much less storage space than regular clothes not only at home, but also while travelling. They are easy to pack, take up little space in the suitcase and and weigh very little. These innovative garments can be machine-washed at 30°C and don't need ironing. As the company focuses on outerwear, their garments are to be worn on top of natural layers. However, they use a range of durable and breathable fabrics. The clothes manufactured by Petit Pli are windproof and waterproof, so children are free to explore the world regardless of the weather.

#10

GOOD DESIGN IS AS LITTLE DESIGN AS POSSIBLE

"Less, but better — because it concentrates on the essential aspects, and the products are not burdened with non-essentials.

Back to purity, back to simplicity."

Dieter Rams

"As little design as possible" is an obvious reference to the credo of the architect Mies van der Rohe: "less is more." Rams adds that "less is only more if it is also better". What are the main aspirations according to the design authority inspired by Japanese philosophy and concepts like wabi-sabi? "We must drastically reduce the chaos of shapes, colours, and symbols that surround us." he states, "We need to defend ourselves against being overwhelmed with stimuli and return to the pure and simple in order to reclaim some leeway for our own selves." Purity and simplicity are at the core of the designs featured in this chapter. Their minimal forms still retain both aesthetic value and practicality. What's more, they resonate perfectly with the spirit of today.

BERNHARDT & VELLA
Vela, 2016 / Arflex

Ellen Bernhardt was born in Germany and Paola Vella in Italy. In 2001, both moved to Milan, where seven years later they started to collaborate. In developing their designs for various manufacturers, they focus on working with simple forms that express the emotions and poetry of objects. They achieve this through a very skilful and sophisticated interplay of shapes and colours. This combination plays a crucial role in the concept of the *Vela* screen designed in 2016 for Arflex. Two gigantic sheets of glass are joined together, complementing each other. The massive scale is counterbalanced by the transparency of the screen and its ability to create interesting shadows. Various combinations of colours in sophisticated hues play with the light to create a cosy, yet elegant, ambience. Also, the unusual contours of *Vela*'s glass panels (each element has a different shape) let it separate the space without limiting or dominating it. The screen gives a feeling of intimacy, but does not cut into the space too much. Instead, it blends into the space, dividing the room smoothly. The fact that the panels are connected in the most minimal way (with a golden metal bar partially running along the height of the construction), adding to the impression that the piece mysteriously floats in the air.

The structure created by the duo Bernhardt & Vella is striking, with a refined beauty. *Vela* is as decorative as it is practical. Screens can tend to be invasive partitions, but here the designers achieved the effect of blending two areas of a space while also dividing it. The irregular silhouettes interplay with the surroundings, instead of being a static element of furnishing. The dynamism of the construction is enhanced by the use of two colours and the intriguing play of shadows they produce in response to light. *Vela*'s purity of form is intensified by the sophisticated choice of interesting shape collisions and colour sequences. Be it a minimalistic room, office or historical interior, *Vela* will perform in any environment. Elegant and simple, it will add lightness to any space due to its barely visible mounting element. Given its discrete construction, subtle hues and classical material, it is also a very unobtrusive design.

RONAN & ERWAN BOUROULLEC
Serif TV, 2015 / Samsung

The French designers and brothers, Ronan and Erwan Bouroullec are famous for their innovative approach to developing any type of design project. Their inventive ideas are executed in a minimalistic style yet still retain the practical aspects of any product. For almost twenty years, this Paris-based design studio has produced many distinctive and well-thought-out creations. Bouroullec's designs have style, character and originality. Active in many fields, their work also encompasses jewellery, furniture, and video as well as spatial arrangements and architecture. Additionally, since the beginning of their career they have been working with the Galerie kreo in Paris to develop more experimental works.

Whatever subject they decide to work on, one is certain that it will be interpreted in an innovative way. The look of the *Serif TV*, which is a collection of screens and televisions designed for Samsung, would convince even the most ardent opponent of TV to buy one for their home. As was its aim, the project indeed pushes the boundaries of what's expected from a television, both aesthetically and technologically. "*Serif* is a television that moves away from a preoccupation with ultra-flat screens." comment the designers. "Instead, it is an object

that can be turned around and manipulated. It can stand anywhere, even on the floor with its own legs. What we were looking for was a solid presence that would sit naturally in various environments, just like an object or a piece of furniture." they add. Its elegant profile when seen from the side, takes the shape of a clear capital "I" (that's also the reason for the name). Its design also allows for a little shelf on the top that can be used for books or trinkets, and a useful base at the bottom so that the screen can sit on any surface, such as a shelf, a piece of furniture or the floor. Users can select between three sizes and three colours to match their interiors. Minimalist in look, the TV is very compact. The smooth back cover is made from magnetic textile and effectively hides all the TV's ports. There is also a special pocket for organizing the cables. The designers have given careful consideration to even the smallest features. The *Serif TV*'s clean lines make it an object of desire so that it acts as an element of decoration in addition to its regular function as a television.

NIKA ZUPANC
Full Moon Lamp, 2013 / Sé London

There is no other designer like Ljubljana-based Nika Zupanc, one of the young super-talents of today. Her works are often called poetic. As she explains, she sees her design as "communicating the things that cannot be told". Whether it is a sofa, a cabinet, a clock or a desk, each design is both feminine and evocative. Another characteristic feature is her attention to every detail, which truly makes a difference, like the motif of a delicate ribbon that appears in many of the works. Zupanc achieves her sophisticated and unique style with simple yet expressive forms. As she states, she "challenges the rational, sober and utilitarian by giving voice to the intuitive, eclectic and intimate". To fulfil her extraordinary concepts, the designer keenly experiments with technologies and materials, making her creations even more fascinating and desirable. Besides working with international manufacturers and fashion houses as well as being involved in various interiors projects, the designer continues to produce objects under her own brand, Nika Zupanc.

While the designer gained international recognition thanks to another beautiful lamp (the *Lolita* lamp developed in 2008 for Moooi), we feature the *Full Moon* Lamp designed 5 years later for Sé London. The lamp exists in two versions, to sit on a table or on the floor, both are supposed to "cast light on our nocturnal worlds". And they do, by echoing the shape of the moon, the lamp's head is circular and flat to resemble the way we see the natural satellite from Earth. This romantic concept is embodied in its very graceful silhouette, which somehow brings a dancing ballerina to mind. The model's base repeats the shape of the flat lamp, just in a much smaller size. The element for adjusting the angle and the switch complements the shape in most discrete way. Zupanc has mastered evoking emotions with just a few elements. *Full Moon* is not only elegant but also highly effective due to its large lighting surface. Made from lacquered aluminium and finished in brass, it is available in black, silver, white and green. All aspects complement the minimal character of the lamp. The design is equally effective in the floor version. The designer, in addition to being very sensible about the form, also has a great sense of proportion.

SEBASTIAN HERKNER
Slot, 2016 / Schönbuch

German designer Sebastian Herkner earned the "someone-to-watch" status some years ago (his ingenious and visually beautiful "Bell Table" designed for ClassiCon in 2012 created a furore in the design world). The signature of the young designer's practise is to combine new technologies with traditional craftsmanship. A graduate in product design from Offenbach University of Art and Design, Herkner established his own studio in 2006. "There is a sensitivity and identity to my work that emphasizes the function, the material and the detail. I transport and interpret characteristics from various contexts of society and culture and implement them in new artifacts." he says about his inspirations, "This character infuses the most everyday objects with respect and personality. In this manner, seemingly contrary things can experience esteem." All these goals Herkner achieves through the use of simple, pure forms, clear design and refined materials.

Slot is yet another inventive concept in Herkner's portfolio. Together with project assistant Betty Montarou, he designed a very minimal, wardrobe system for the brand Schönbuch. The purity of the geometrical forms is striking, as is also true in the practicality of the idea. The two types of elongated and round panels, mounted to the wall with steel spacer rods, are very light, but can accommodate a lot of clothes. Both types of module can be individually arranged according to the user's needs and available space. The longer elements obviously hide more, but the interplay between them and the round ones, especially when they have different finishes, gives an interesting look. To make the structure even more useful, the front panels, which are available in a wide range of matt and high-gloss paint colours, can also be equipped with a mirror. In addition, the system can be used as a coat rack in the entrance hall, where a quick glance into a mirror is essential. *Slot* seems like the perfect solution for rooms with limited space, where a traditional wardrobe is not a possibility (or in hotels, for that matter). Light and elegant, it can be a very decorative and visually discrete element in any space. The simplicity of the geometrical forms is in tune with the refined way that they are finished. The rounded shapes deceptively suspend in the air, blending into the surroundings.

CLAESSON KOIVISTO RUNE
Biru, 2017 / Smaller Objects

      Stockholm-based Claesson Koivisto Rune was founded in 1995 as an architectural partnership by Mårten Claesson, Eero Koivisto and Ola Rune (all graduates of Konstfack University College of Arts, Crafts and Design in Stockholm). Over time they have developed into a multi-disciplinary practice working with numerous manufacturers around the world. The range of designs spans tableware, textiles, lighting, electronics, furniture as well as buildings, offices, shops and hotels, among other areas. They received many prestigious awards for their designs. Scandinavian flair meets with practical solutions and innovative forms in their works. Although every project is completely different from the next, each reflects the trio's style. A combination of geometry and vivid colours plays an important role in their creations, whether big or small. The objects designed by the studio are gently rounded to evoke a cosy ambience (even if some of the tiles or carpets have sharp edges, their patterns are selected to soften the visual impression). Simplicity and purity are at the core of many of their works.

The *Biru* (the Japanese word for beer) is a minimalistic bottle opener that is based on a geometrical order. To obtain the harmonic figure, the designers combined a superellipse* with a supercircle. Their goal was to develop a simple shape that sits perfectly in the palm of the hand (its diameter is 7 cm). It is totally functional, making opening a bottle easy and quick. *Biru*'s balanced form is further emphasised by the use of a basic material, stainless steel. The bottle opener was designed for the label Smaller Objects, established by the three designers in 2015. It focuses on a wide range of useful design objects for the home made in wool, ceramics, wood or steel.

*The trio explains: "The French mathematician Gabriel Lamé first described the formula of the superellipse. Danish poet and scientist Piet Hein found practical use for it. Swedish architect and designer Bruno Mathsson refined it into the famous Superellipse table. What is less well known is that Piet Hein, in collaboration with architect David Helldén, designed Stockholm's central square, Sergels Torg, using the superellipse, or perhaps more accurately, the supercircle, for the defining traffic circle. In its presentation, Hein wrote: "Things made with straight lines fit well together and save space. And we can move easily around things made with round lines. But we are in a straightjacket, having to accept one or the other. The superellipse solves the problem. It's neither nor. Yet it is definite — it has unity."

LAYER / BENJAMIN HUBERT
Disruptive Devices, 2017 / nolii

Layer, a strategic industrial design agency, was established by a young British designer, Benjamin Hubert. "From app design and the next generation of wearables to smart domestic appliances, fast moving consumer goods, and intelligent furniture systems, we create products that meet the demands of tomorrow today." Layer states. The team's golden rules include: thoughtful storytelling (to turn user experience into a way of life), simple statements (by identifying only the essential to eliminate the visual noise and all that's unnecessary), functional intelligence (understood as the ability to effectively improve the everyday), meaningful materiality (materials should evoke a powerful emotional response) and creativity with a conscience (objects should be designed with a minimal environmental impact). Nolii is a new technology brand, which Hubert co-founded with tech entrepreneur Asad Hamir.

Disruptive devices, developed in 2017 for nolii, is the quintessence of Layer's philosophy. This desirable collection was invented with technologically advanced users in mind. To make everyday life with their devices easy, Layer invented a whole collection of multi-functional products that enable "users to stay connected effortlessly". As we all know, technology only theoretically improves our lifestyles, in reality many devices we use on a regular basis mean the constant need to recharge low batteries or transfer files, among other complications. Layer's solutions solve many users' headaches and provide a smooth co-existence with our laptops, mobiles, tablets etc. "From chaotic cords and broken cables to limited charging solutions, our lives are too often interrupted by everyday tech challenges." says the designer. Insightful research fuels these high-performance products, which work alone or together. Charging cables, back slots for accessories, compact plugs and on-the-go chargers, in short, all the tech essentials we need, are elegantly hidden in simple, sleek shelves. This is a versatile collection for today as well as tomorrow when we will be even more dependent on technology. It is pure in look and perfectly functional. The designer has included only the essentials, none of the elements is superfluous yet it is equipped with everything needed. Its minimal design is totally unobtrusive and, what's most important, very handy. Available in several colour versions, the elements of the collection can be used individually or mixed to create interesting combinations.

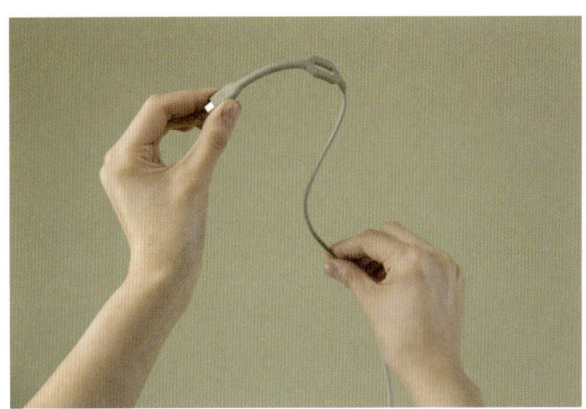

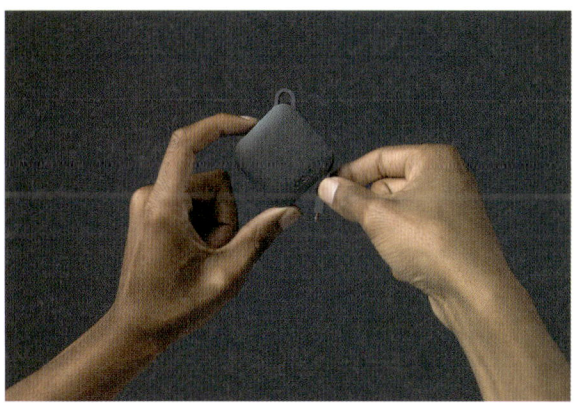
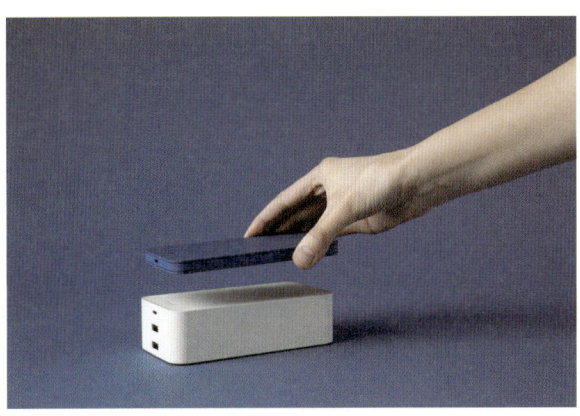
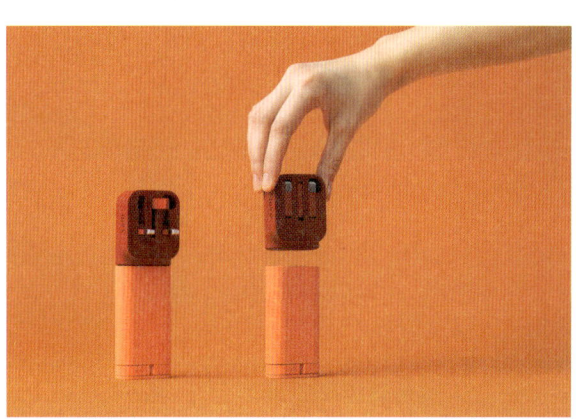

EDWARD BARBER & JAY OSGERBY
Piton Stool, 2015 / Knoll

If there was one feature that could describe the practice of Edward Barber and Jay Osgerby, both graduates of Architecture at The Royal College of Art in London, it would be a no-philosophy of avoiding sharp-lines. Whether these are the legs of a table, coat hangers, sofa cushions or lamps, their edges are soft and the shapes rounded. In effect, the objects complement their surrounding, there is a sense of fluidity. The forms that Barber & Osgerby play with are minimalistic, but at the same time each element is very human and harmonious. The duo established their studio in 1996 and much of their early work, as they remark, "involved the folding and shaping of sheet material, influenced by the white card that they had used frequently in architectural model making". Whatever material they decide to use in their creations, be it wood, upholstery or paper, the designers turn it into visually shapely designs.

A stool is a practical piece of furniture, but usually not very original in design or perhaps regarded as unworthy of special attention. Barber & Osgerby proved this wrong with their *Piton Stool* designed for Knoll, which makes a nice exception. The designers delivered an elegant and graceful piece of furniture that is as useful as it is aesthetically pleasing. Made of robust cast aluminium, *Piton* is finished with durable powder coat paint so it is equally suitable for outdoor use. "The geometric, elementary framework of the base is an interpretation of the familiar tripod structure," the designers comment, "its tripod legs visually are contained by two rings." All elements are well proportioned. The repetition of the circle and rhythmic arrangement of the legs give an impression of harmonious dynamism. A stool turns into a surprising structure that can add a nice accent to any space. The height can be easily adjusted thanks to a screw mechanism beneath the seat so Piton is very easy to use (and to move for that matter due to its light structure). The model is also available in a range of vivid colours. Barber & Osgerby used the same concept on a larger scale to develop a side table in the same series.

MICHAËL VERHEYDEN
Gullring Crystal Vase

In his interview for the *New York Times*, Belgian designer Michaël Verheyden, states: "I'm not a New-Age-y guy, but it's something I strive for, to be very Zen." His designs are extremely minimalist, not only because of their pure forms but also due to the materials the designer chooses to work with, such as marble or glass. After studying industrial design at the Media & Design Academy in Genk plus working as a model and doing some designs for Raf Simons, Verheyden launched his own line in 2002. Starting with handbags, he decided to expand the scope of his work and began designing home accessories as well as furniture, joined by his wife Saartje Vereecke. Geometry plays an important role in Verheyden's creations. Harmonious and well-thought-out forms are executed in classical yet expressive materials. This combination embues each object with lots of character and timeless beauty.

The devil is in the detail, which in this case would be the proportions between the crystal and bronze elements in the *Gullring Crystal Vase* (not to mention the striking formal purity). The sleek ring sitting at the top of the elongated body of the solid crystal vase is a sublime finish. It looks as if it was suspended in air. As in his other designs, Verheyden has created an elegant and imaginative juxtaposition of the highest quality materials. While the formal purity is very expressive, the vase's straightforward silhouette is captivating and in line with the designer's aesthetic of basic forms. The effect is a clean and visually powerful design.

Gullring seems to be perfect for either a bunch of flowers or a single stem. It cries out for a flower that would be equally elegant and unique. As with his other objects, this vase was also finished, assembled and packaged in Verheyden's studio. The designer is known for personally making prototypes of his designs and working closely with crafts experts to finalise the production. Timeless beauty and classical elegance meet in the *Gullring*, which fosters sophisticated minimalism in how to exhibit flowers.

DAVID MELLOR
Minimal Cutlery, 2003

The late David Mellor, Royal Designer for Industry, embraced an unusual combination of craftsman (he was originally trained as a silversmith) and design activities in his practice. He found it important to enable him to supervise each product through every stage from concept to customer. Mellor's main ambition was to improve design standards and directly affect many people's lives, which he successfully did throughout his long career. Beginning with one-off pieces of silver, over time he broadened the spectrum of his designs to become famous for many ranges of stainless steel and silver cutlery. These have been manufactured for many years in his own purpose-built factory in Derbyshire (the company is now led by the designer's son Corin, who continues creating new designs). Interestingly, Mellor was commissioned by the government to realise many important projects, such as redesigning the national traffic light system (which is still in use today) or a new square post box (this one caused some controversies). As a craftsman, he put a strong emphasis on materials and techniques in his work.

This approach is evident in the *Minimal cutlery* from 2003, which is claimed to be the designer's most innovative cutlery. The place setting consists of five pieces: a knife, a fork and three different spoons, and a large serving spoon is also available in the series. Praised for its aesthetic purity, it was developed as a modern living tool. The design was such a success that it was not only popular among the customers, but also produced in huge quantities for British government canteens and NHS hospitals. Made of the highest quality stainless steel, satin polished, the set is an interesting visual game between the glossy and matt surfaces, particularly visible due to its simple forms. The shaping of all parts of the set is very sculptural, but the most original form is the one-piece knife. Innovative and beautiful, the Mellor's set sits well in the hand. The design oscillates between minimal forms and rich material, which gives a powerful look to these everyday tools.

PATRICIA URQUIOLA
Rotazioni, 2017 / cc-tapis
Visioni, 2016 / cc-tapis

Patricia Urquiola is one of those contemporary designers who do not need a special introduction. Spanish-born and Milan-based, Urquiola is particularly gifted at creating ingenious and aesthetically beautiful solutions. Realising numerous interior design commissions and designing for the leading international manufacturers, the designer has run her own studio since 2001. Acting as an art director for Cassina, she is also responsible for the new product development office of DePadova. In the past she worked with Vico Magistretti, as head of Lissoni Associati's design group. Her concepts whether her product or interior design are always fresh, captivating and express the spirit of today. "I always remember Achille Castiglioni, one of my mentors," she says, "and he always said that in industrial design you have the idea, the fantasy, the concept — that's the marmalade. But the constraint of the brief is the bread. You need both in order to find structure for your ideas." Urquiola adds. Her amazing designs definitely have both.

Geometry dominates Urquiola's two-piece collection of graphic rugs. *Visioni* combines rectangles of different shapes, while *Rotazioni* displays repetitive cylindrical shapes. Both compositions are very plastic and dynamic. The shapes combine in contrasting pastel colours defined by sharp black contours. Thanks to this, these perfectly flat surfaces seem to flow. Moreover, the abstract patterns on the rugs, both the superimposed cylinders and architectural rectangles, introduce a curious perspective within the interior by deceiving the eye (an almost trompe d'oeil effect) whether it is placed on the floor or hung on the wall. The bold design is achieved here with a simple yet imaginative game of optical illusion and repetition of basic geometrical forms. Both rugs were designed for cc-tapis and are a perfect fusion of modern design and the highest-quality craftsmanship. The company established initially in France, moved to Milan in 2011. They are famous for bringing innovation to rug design through a new approach to traditional methods. Their contemporary hand-knotted rugs are created by world-renowned designers and made in Nepal by expert Tibetan artisans with a strong respect for the ancient craft and material, which in this case is the softest Himalayan wool.

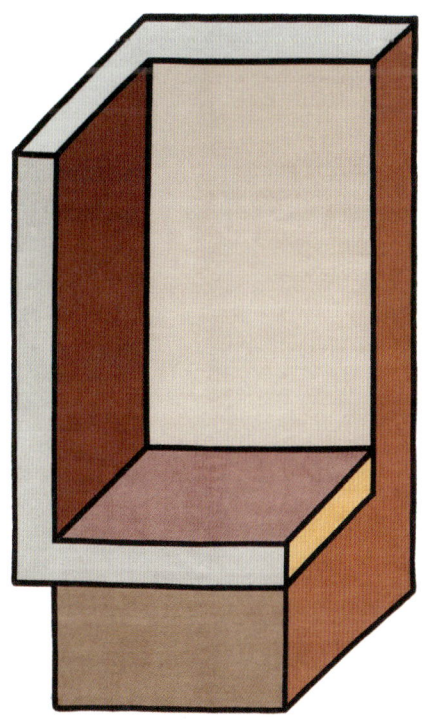

DESIGNERS

DAVID ADJAYE adjaye.com
TOMÁS ALONSO tomas-alonso.com
ANDERSSEN & VOLL anderssen-voll.com
TADAO ANDO tadao-ando.com
AYTM aytm.dk
FRANÇOIS AZAMBOURG azambourg.com
ALDO BAKKER aldobakker.com
EDWARD BARBER & JAY OSGERBY
barberosgerby.com
YVES BÉHAR fuseproject.com
THOMAS BENTZEN thomasbentzen.com
BERNHARDT & VELLA bernhardt-vella.com
THOMAS BERNSTRAND + LINDAU & BORSELIUS
bernstrand.com   borselius.se
LARA BOHINC bohincstudio.com
RONAN & ERWAN BOUROULLEC
bouroullec.com
BOWER STUDIOS bower-studios.com
ANNE BOYSEN anneboysen.dk
CRISTINA CELESTINO cristinacelestino.com
NEWDEALDESIGN newdealdesign.com
CLAESSON KOIVISTO RUNE claessonkoivistorune.se
MATALI CRASSET matalicrasset.com
MARK DAY
DECHEM STUDIO dechemstudio.com
PAULINE DELTOUR paulinedeltour.com
GUILLAUME DELVIGNE guillaumedelvigne.com
STEFAN DIEZ diezoffice.com
TOM DIXON tomdixon.net
DOSHI LEVIEN doshilevien.com
NOÉ DUCHAUFOUR-LAWRANCE
noeduchaufourlawrance.com
E15 e15.com
EOOS eoos.com
MARTIN ERICSSON martinericsson.se
FORMAFANTASMA formafantasma.com
MONICA FÖRSTER monicaforster.se
SOU FUJIMOTO sou-fujimoto.net
FRONT DESIGN frontdesign.se
GAMFRATESI gamfratesi.com
KONSTANTIN GRCIC konstantin-grcic.com
CONSTANCE GUISSET constanceguisset.com

JAIME HAYON hayonstudio.com
ROBIN HEATHER aberja.net
HEATHERWICK STUDIO heatherwick.com
SEBASTIAN HERKNER sebastianherkner.com
CONSTANTINOS HOURSOGLOU
hoursoglou.com
BENJAMIN HUBERT layerdesign.com
JEHS+LAUB jehs-laub.com
HELLA JONGERIUS jongeriuslab.com
CHARLOTTE JUILLARD charlottejuillard.com
JIN JURAMOTO jinkuramoto.com
KEISUKE KAWASE keisukekawase.info
HARRI KOSKINEN harrikoskinen.com
TOMAS KRAL tomaskral.ch
ANTOINE LESUR antoinelesur.com
ARIK LEVY ariklevy.fr
KAI LINKE kailinke.com
MLADEN HOYSS AND ADHAM BADR blloc.com
EMANUELE MAGINI emanuelemagini.it
CECILIE MANZ ceciliemanz.com
Stéphanie Marin/SMARIN smarin.net
DAVID MELLOR davidmellordesign.com
ALESSANDRO MENDINI ateliermendini.it
JASPER MORRISON jaspermorrison.com
NENDO nendo.jp
NERI & HU neriandhu.com
NEW TENDENCY newtendency.com
NICHETTO STUDIO nichettostudio.com
PHILIPPE NIGRO philippenigro.com
NORM ARCHITECTS normcph.com
NORMAL STUDIO normalstudio.fr
NATHALIE DU PASQUIER
nathaliedupasquier.com
HENRIK PEDERSEN
FEDERICO PEPE ledictateur.com
KARIM RASHID karimrashid.com
PIETRO RUSSO pietrorusso.com
LENA SALEH lenasaleh.com
ADAM SAVAGE adamsavage.com
INGA SEMPÉ ingasempe.fr
SHANE SCHNECK officefordesign.se
SCHOLTEN & BAIJINGS scholtenbaijings.com
BRIAN SIRONI briansironi.it
JULIEN DE SMEDT jdsa.eu

MICHAEL SODEAU michaelsodeau.com
SOVRAPPENSIERO DESIGN STUDIO
sovrappensiero.com
ELISA STROZYK elisastrozyk.de
STUDIO ORIJEEN orijeen.com
SUPER LOCAL super-local.com
SWNA theswna.com
PATRICIA URQUIOLA patriciaurquiola.com
MARJAN VAN AUBEL marjanvanaubel.com
ROGER VANCELLS rogervancells.com
EVANGELOS VASILEIOU evangelosvasileiou.com
MARC VENOT marc-venot.com
MICHAËL VERHEYDEN michaelverheyden.be
CLARA VON ZWEIGBERGK
claravonzweigbergk.se
CHRISTIAN WERNER christian-werner.com
RYAN MARIO YASIN ryanmarioyasin.com
YUUE yuuedesign.com
NIKA ZUPANC nikazupanc.com

MANUFACTURERS

Adidas Adidas.com
Alias alias.design
antoniolupi antoniolupi.it
Arflex arflex.it
Atelier Swarovski Home
atelierswarovski.com/home-decor
Axor axor-design.com
Blå Station blastation.com
Blloc blloc.com
bobble waterbobble.com
Bomma bomma.cz
Bosa bosatrade.com
by | n
Caventou caventou.com
cc-tapis cc-tapis.com
Concrete LCDA concrete-beton.com
Cristal de Sèvres cristalsevres.com
Davis davisfurniture.com
Dote Dote.co
Ecopixel ecopixel.eu
Editions Milano editionsmilano.com
Erik Jørgensen erik-joergensen.com

Genano genano.com
Gloster Furniture GmbH gloster.com
Gufram gufram.it
HAY hay.dk
Herman Miller hermanmiller.com
Hermès hermes.com
Ichendorf Milano ichendorfmilano.com
Interlübke interluebke.com
Knoll, Inc knoll.com
Korea Gyeonggido Company
Kvadrat kvadrat.de
LAMY lamy.com
Ligne Roset ligne-roset.com
Made Design
MAFIA Bags mafiabags.com
Marsotto Edizioni edizioni.marsotto.com
Master & Dynamic masterdynamic.com
Menu menu.as
MINIMALUX minimalux.com
Muuto muuto.com
NATIVE UNION nativeunion.com
nolii wearenolii.com
Nude Glass nudeglass.com
NUKI nuki.io
Offecct offecct.com
Petit Pli petitpli.com
Poltrona Frau poltronafrau.com
Rubberband rubberbandproducts.com
Samsung samsung.com
Schönbuch schoenbuch.com
Sé London se-collections.com
Shibui shibui.ch
SIMPLEHUMAN simplehuman.com
Smaller Objects smallerobjects.com
Tex, Carrefour
Texturae texturae.it
Tubes tubesradiatori.com
Venini venini.com
Vestre vestre.com
VIA PLATTEN viaplatten.de
Vitra vitra.com
Wittmann wittmann.at

PHOTO CREDITS

pp. 003 © Vitsœ; 006-007 © Blloc; 008-009 © Hermann Miller; 010-011 © NewDealDesign; 013 © NATIVE UNION; 014-015 © Nichetto Studio; 016-017 © Yuue; 019 © Nuki; 020-021 © Lena Saleh; 022-023 courtesy Pauline Deltour, © @yellowinnovation; 024-025 © simplehuman; 028-031 courtesy of nendo, photos © Akihiro Yoshida; 032-033 © Ligne Roset; 034-035 © HeatherwickStudio; 036-037 © SWNA, © Korea Gyeonggido Company; 039 © Ligne Roset; 040-041 courtesy of Constantinos Hoursoglou, photo © Nikos Alexopoulos; 042-043 © Philippe Nigro; 044-045 © Vitra; 046-047 courtesy of Keisuke Kawase, photo: © Yoshihito Kagami; 048-049 © Minimalux.com; 052-053 © Bomma; 054-055 courtesy of Noé Duchaufour-Lawrance, photo © Nuno Sousa Dias; 056-057 © Orijeen; 058-059 © Wittmann; 060-061 © Editions Milano; 062-063 © Courtesy of Swarovski; 064 © Front Design; 066-067 © Formafantasma, © Nude Glass; 068-069 © Neri&Hu, © Poltrona Frau; 070-071 courtesy of Rubberband, photo © Vihan Shah; 074-075 © Bosa; 076-077 © interlübke; 078-079 © Sou Fujimoto Architects, © Alias; 080-081 © Muuto; 082-083 © Tomas Kral; 084-085 courtesy of Guillaume Delvigne, photos © Alain Gelberger; 086-087 © Emanuele Magini; 088-092 © Hay; 093 © C.v.Z. Studio; 096-097 © Muuto; 098-099 © Hay; 100-101 courtesy of Marsotto Edizioni, photo © Miro Zagnoli; 102-103 © New Tendency; 104-105 courtesy of Julien De Smedt, photo © Vestre; 106-107 © Lamy; 108-109 © Davis Furniture; 110-111 © Genano; 112-113 courtesy of Martic Ericcson, photo p. 113 © Jan Holmgren; 114-115 © Gloster Furniture GmbH; 119 © Wittmann; 121 © Ligne Roset; 122-123 © Vitra; 124-125 © aytm.dk; 126-127 courtesy of Blå Station, photos © Erik Karlsson; 128-129 © Hay; 130-131 courtesy of Matali Crasset, photos © Julien Jouanjus; 132-133 © Made Design® Barcelona, © Roger Vancells; 134-135 © Marc Venot; 136-137 © Starling Bank; 140-141 © Ligne Roset; 142-143 © Norm Architects; 144-145 © NORMAL STUDIO; 146-147 courtesy of Bower Studios, photos © Charlie Schuck; 148-149 © Master & Dynamic; 150-151 © smarin; 152-153 © e15; 154-155 courtesy of Tom Dixon, photos © Peer Lindgreen; 156-157 courtesy of Robin Heather & Kai Linke, photos © VIA GmbH; 158-159 © Editions Milano; 162-163 © Lara Bohinc; 164-165 © Muuto; 166-167 © Kvadrat; 168-169 © Erik Jørgensen; 170-171 © Hay; 172 courtesy of Swarovski, 173 courtesy of Mark Cocksedge; 175 © Venini; 176 © SOVRAPPENSIERO DESIGN STUDIO, © Texturae; 178-179 courtesy of Elisa Strozyk, photos © STUDIO BEEN; 180-181 courtesy of Cristina Celestino, photo p.180 © Alberto Strada; 184-185 © Offecct; 186-189 © ecopixel; 190-191 courtesy of Super Local, photos p. 190 © Jeroen van der Wielen, p. 191 © Pim van Baarsen; 192-193 © Adidas, 194-195 courtesy of Marjan van Aubel, photos © Sasa Stucin / Amy Gwatkin; 196-197 © Dote; 198-199 courtesy of Adam Savage, photo © Norman Chan; 200-201 courtesy of Karim Rashid; 202-203 © antoniolupi; 204-205 © Ryan Mario Yasin; 208-209 © Arflex; 210-211 © Ronan & Erwan Bouroullec – 2004; 212-213 courtesy of Nika Zupanc photos © Sé London; 214-215 © Sebastian Herkner; 216-217 © CLAESSON KOIVISTO RUNE; 219-221 © Layer | Benjamin Hubert for nolii; 222-223 Courtesy of Knoll, Inc.; 225 courtesy of Michaël Verheyden, photo © Frederic Vercruysse; 226-227 © David Mellor Design; 228-231 courtesy cc-tapis, photos p. 230-231 by © Lorenzo Gironi - Styling Motel409

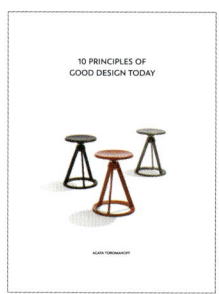

pp. 222 Piton Stool © Knoll